Editor
Stephanie Buehler, Psy. D.

Editorial Project Manager
Ina Massler Levin, M.A.

Editor-in-Chief
Sharon Coan, M.S. Ed.

Illustrator
Chandler Sinnott

Cover Artist
Denise Bauer

Art Coordinator
Denice Adorno

Creative Director
Rich D'Sa

Imaging
Ralph Olmedo, Jr.

Product Manager
Phil Garcia

Publisher
Mary D. Smith, M.S. Ed.

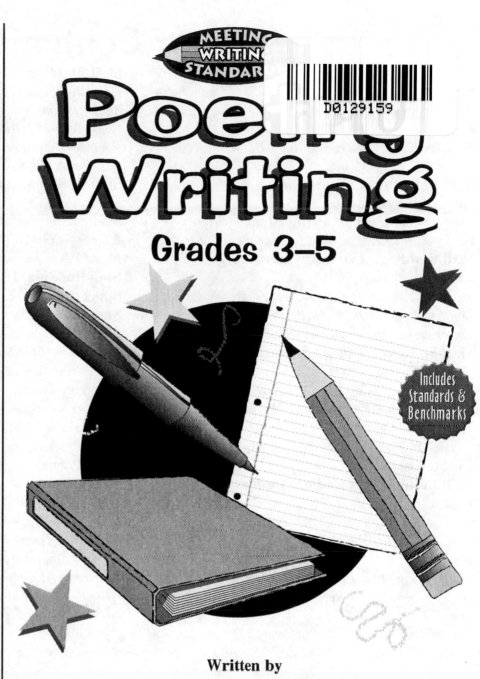

Poetry Writing

Grades 3–5

Includes Standards & Benchmarks

Written by

Kimberly A. Williams

Teacher Created Resources, Inc.
6421 Industry Way
Westminster, CA 92683
www.teachercreated.com

ISBN: 978-1-57690-992-8

©2000 Teacher Created Resources, Inc.
Reprinted, 2010
Made in U.S.A.

Table of Contents

How to Use This Book

"Yuck! Not poetry!"

"I hate poetry. It's stupid."

"I don't know how to write a poem."

Sound familiar? Many students (and some teachers) have had negative experiences with poetry. Poetry is seen as being too hard, too boring, or too silly. (Sound like the vocabulary of your students?) This book is for teachers who want to teach poetry to their students but who don't know either how to begin or how to present the lessons and still maintain student excitement and motivation.

Poetry Writing presents developmentally-arranged lessons for both teaching different types of poems and the skills necessary to write them. Activities for generating topics for poetry are presented in the beginning of the book. Eight different poetry techniques are explained in skill-building lessons. Activities designed to help students master standards described and listed on pages 4–6 are included with each lesson.

Lessons for teaching 18 different types of poems are contained in the book. Each lesson provides a definition of the poem type for the teacher, a list of the requisite skills needed by the students, and materials to be prepared prior to the lesson implementation. The lessons lead students through each stage of the writing process. Time-saving student reproducibles are incorporated into the lessons. Samples of exemplary student writing are also included as models for students. For each different poem that students write, a response sheet for peer, self, and teacher evaluation is also included. Ideas for writing across the curriculum are given for each type of poem on pages labeled *Curriculum Connections*. The Curriculum Connections are designed to be copied onto card stock and kept together in a card file box.

As a culminating activity, reproducibles that lead students through the process of creating a poetry collection are presented. Throughout the publishing stages for each poem and for the poetry collection, students are encouraged to use technology or present their poems with creativity and color.

Hopefully, both you and your students will enjoy and grow from the lessons presented in this book.

Standards for Writing
Grades 3–5

Accompanying the major activities of this book will be references to the basic standards and benchmarks for writing that will be met by successful performance of the activities. Each specific standard and benchmark will be referred to by the appropriate letter and number from the following collection. For example, a basic standard and benchmark identified as **1A** would be as follows:

> **Standard 1:** Demonstrates competence in the general skills and strategies of the writing process
>
> **Benchmark A:** Prewriting: Uses prewriting strategies to plan written work (e.g., uses graphic organizers, story maps, and webs; groups related ideas; takes notes; brainstorms ideas)

A basic standard and benchmark identified as **4B** would be as follows:

> **Standard 4:** Gathers and uses information for research purposes
>
> **Benchmark B**: Uses encyclopedias to gather information for research topics

Clearly, some activities will address more than one standard. Moreover, since there is a rich supply of activities included in this book, some will overlap in the skills they address, and some, of course, will not address every single benchmark within a given standard. Therefore, when you see these standards referenced in the activities, refer to this section for complete descriptions.

Although virtually every state has published its own standards and every subject area maintains its own lists, there is surprising commonality among these various sources. For the purposes of this book, we have elected to use the collection of standards synthesized by John S. Kendall and Robert J. Marzano in their book *Content Knowledge: A Compendium of Standards and Benchmarks for K–12 Education* (Second Edition, 1997) as illustrative of what students at various grade levels should know and be able to do. The book is published jointly by McREL (Mid-continent Regional Educational Laboratory, Inc.) and ASCD (Association for Supervision and Curriculum Development). (Used by permission of McREL.)

Writing:

1. Demonstrates competence in the general skills and strategies of the writing process
2. Demonstrates competence in the stylistic and rhetorical aspects of writing
3. Uses grammatical and mechanical conventions in written compositions
4. Gathers and uses information for research purposes

Level II (Grades 3–5)

> **1. Demonstrates competence in the general skills and strategies of the writing process**

A. Prewriting: Uses prewriting strategies to plan written work (e.g., uses graphic organizers, story maps, and webs; groups related ideas; takes notes; brainstorms ideas)

B. Drafting and Revising: Uses strategies to draft and revise written work (e.g., elaborates on a central idea; writes with attention to voice, audience, word choice, tone and imagery; uses paragraphs to develop separate ideas)

Standards for Writing *(cont.)*
Grades 3–5

C. Editing and Publishing: Uses strategies to edit and publish written work (e.g., edits for grammar, punctuation, capitalization, and spelling at a developmentally appropriate level; considers page format [paragraphs, margins, indentations, titles]; selects presentation format; incorporates photos, illustrations, charts, and graphs)

D. Evaluates own and others' writing (e.g., identifies the best features of a piece of writing, determines how own writing achieves its purposes, asks for feedback, responds to classmates' writing)

E. Writes stories or essays that show awareness of intended audience

F. Writes stories or essays that convey an intended purpose (e.g., to record ideas, to describe, to explain)

G. Writes expository compositions (e.g., identifies and stays on the topic; develops the topic with simple facts, details, examples, and explanations; excludes extraneous and inappropriate information)

H. Writes narrative accounts (e.g., engages the reader by establishing a context and otherwise creates an organizational structure that balances and unifies all narrative aspects of the story; uses sensory details and concrete language to develop plot and character; uses a range of strategies such as dialogue and tension or suspense)

I. Writes autobiographical compositions (e.g., provides a context within which the incident occurs, uses simple narrative strategies, provides some insight into why this incident is memorable)

J. Writes expressive compositions (e.g., expresses ideas, reflections, and observations; uses an individual, authentic voice; uses narrative strategies, relevant details, and ideas that enable the reader to imagine the world of the event or experience)

K. Writes in response to literature (e.g., advances judgements; supports judgements with references to the text, other works, other authors, nonprint media, and personal knowledge)

L. Writes personal letters (e.g., includes the date, address, greeting, and closing; addresses envelopes)

2. Demonstrates competence in the stylistic and rhetorical aspects of writing

A. Uses descriptive language that clarifies and enhances ideas (e.g., describes familiar people, places, or objects)

B. Uses paragraph form in writing (e.g., indents the first word of a paragraph, uses topic sentences, recognizes a paragraph as a group of sentences about one main idea, writes several related paragraphs)

C. Uses a variety of sentence structures

3. Uses grammatical and mechanical conventions in written compositions

A. Writes in cursive

B. Uses exclamatory and imperative sentences in written compositions

Standards for Writing (cont.)
Grades 3–5

C. Uses pronouns in written compositions (e.g., substitutes pronouns for nouns)

D. Uses nouns in written compositions (e.g., uses plural and singular naming words; forms regular and irregular plurals of nouns; uses common and proper nouns; uses nouns as subjects)

E. Uses verbs in written compositions (e.g., uses a wide variety of action verbs, past and present verb tenses, simple tenses, forms of regular verbs, verbs that agree with the subject)

F. Uses adjectives in written compositions (e.g., indefinite, numerical, predicate adjectives)

G. Uses adverbs in written compositions (e.g., to make comparisons)

H. Uses coordinating conjunctions in written compositions (e.g., links ideas using connecting words)

I. Uses negatives in written compositions (e.g., avoids double negatives)

J. Uses conventions of spelling in written compositions (e.g., spells high frequency, commonly misspelled words from appropriate grade-level list; uses a dictionary and other resources to spell words; uses initial consonant substitution to spell related words; uses vowel combinations for correct spelling)

K. Uses conventions of capitalization in written compositions (e.g., titles of people; proper nouns [names of towns, cities, counties, and states; days of the week; months of the year; names of streets; names of countries; holidays]; first word of direct quotations; heading, salutation, and closing of a letter)

L. Uses conventions of punctuation in written compositions (e.g., uses periods after imperative sentences and in initials, abbreviations, and titles before names; uses commas in dates and addresses and after greetings and closings in a letter; uses apostrophes in contractions and possessive nouns; uses quotation marks around titles and with direct quotations; uses a colon between hours and minutes)

4. Gathers and uses information for research purposes

A. Uses a variety of strategies to identify topics to investigate (e.g., brainstorms, lists questions, uses idea webs)

B. Uses encyclopedias to gather information for research topics

C. Uses dictionaries to gather information for research topics

D. Uses key words, indexes, cross-references, and letters on volumes to find information for research topics

E. Uses multiple representations of information (e.g., maps, charts, photos) to find information for research topics

F. Uses graphic organizers to gather and record information for research topics (e.g., notes, charts, graphs)

G. Compiles information into written reports or summaries

Poetry Dictionary

Students need to become familiar with several different terms related to poetry. Providing students with a poetry dictionary helps them keep track of the new vocabulary they learn during the unit.

You may choose to use the poetry dictionary in several different ways. Some teachers provide students with the terms and the definitions at the beginning of the unit and review the terms with students as they encounter them in their writing lessons. Others prefer to provide students with a blank sheet of terms and then define the terms for students as they progress through the unit. Either way, students gain an understanding of the terms as they relate to poetry and are held accountable for including several of the techniques and terms in their poems.

Terms for a Poetry Dictionary

alliteration: words beginning with the same consonant sound
(Example: In summer the sun is strong.)

formula poetry: poems that follow a specified formula or pattern (Examples: haiku, diamante)

free verse: poems that can be written as the author chooses; they do not follow a specified rhyme scheme or pattern
(Examples: snapshot poem, event poem)

imagery: a mental picture

metaphor: comparing two things without using *like* or *as*
(Example: Paul Bunyan is a mountain of a man.)

onomatopoeia: use of words to represent or imitate sounds
(Example: The *boom* of the thunder woke me from my nap.)

poetry: words arranged in such a way as to express ideas and emotions.

repetition: repeating the same words or phrases in a line or a poem
(Example: There once was a boy *from Mars, from Mars* Who liked to work *on cars, on cars.* . . .)

rhyme: when two or more words have the same sound
(Example: I'm not going to school *today* I'd rather go outside and *play.* . . .)

rhythm: a regular pattern of accented and unaccented syllables
(Example: A little old man from *Peru,* Was sailing a ship with his *crew.* . . .)

simile: comparing two things using *like* or *as*
(Example: Paul Bunyan is as big as a mountain.)

stanza: a number of lines that divide a poem into sections

Generating Ideas: Fast-Writes

Background for the Teacher

Materials: 4" x 6" (10 cm x 15 cm) index cards (10 per student), a letter-sized envelope for each student, an egg timer or other timekeeper

Lesson Plan

1. Distribute 10 index cards and one envelope to each student.

2. Explain to students that they will be generating ideas for writing poetry, using a technique called "fast-writing." Once you give them a topic, they are to write as fast as they can for one minute to generate a list of ideas on the topic. The goal is to list as many ideas as possible on the topic before time is called.

3. Inform students of the first topic, set the timer for one minute, and instruct students to "Go!" After one minute, call time and have students stop writing on that topic. At this point, tell students to write the topic on their index card since they did not have an opportunity to do so before writing.

4. Continue in this manner until students have written on each topic. Students should use a new index card for each topic. When they are finished, students should write their name on the outside of their envelope and keep the cards in the envelope. You may wish to collect all the envelopes and keep them in a file box in the classroom for easy reference and safe-keeping.

Suggested Fast-Write Topics

1. your favorite things

2. favorite childhood memories

3. things that make you angry or upset

4. things in nature that you think are pretty

5. things you know about that most people don't

6. things you hate

7. people who are important to you

8. words that describe you

9. things that disgust you

10. things you couldn't live without

Generating Ideas:
Poet Tree Bulletin Board

Background for the Teacher

Materials: brown bulletin board paper cut into the shape of a large tree trunk with bare branches; leaf patterns completed with writing ideas (see pages 9–10) copied onto green, yellow, red, brown, or orange construction paper and laminated for durability; bulletin board letters for the title, "Pick From the Poet Tree"; Velcro dots (optional)

Lesson Presentation

1. Staple the bare tree trunk shape to the bulletin board.

2. Staple the leaf cut-outs to the tree. Attach the leaves so that students are able to read the writing ideas written on each of the leaves. You may wish to attach the leaves with Velcro so that students can remove a leaf and take it back to their desks to write.

3. Allow students to use the bulletin board to generate unusual topics for their poetry.

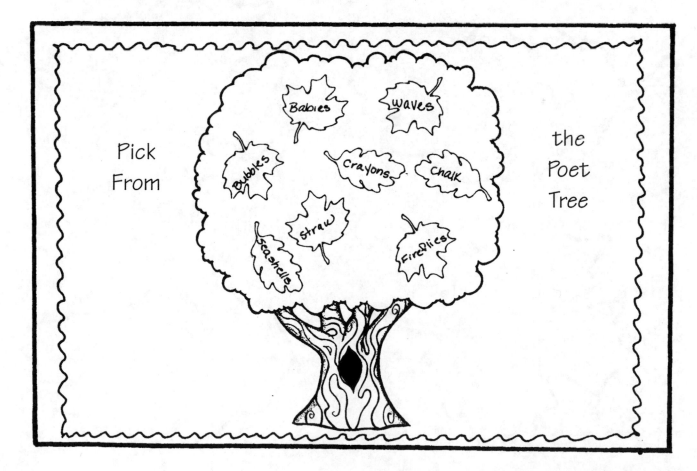

Poet Tree Bulletin Board *(cont.)*

Copy the leaf patterns onto green, orange, red, brown, and yellow paper. Write the suggested topics onto the leaves, cut them out, and attach them around the construction paper tree trunk on your "Pick from the Poet Tree" bulletin board with pins or Velcro dots (see page 9).

Suggested Topics for the Poet Tree Bulletin Board

- rainbows
- an electric eel
- fireflies
- fleas
- shoelaces
- sandboxes
- toilets
- sharks
- TV

- ear wax
- rubber bands
- sandpaper
- a car wash
- flip-flops
- bubbles
- sunburn
- stained-glass windows
- make-up

- a cuckoo clock
- refried beans
- anthills
- bandages
- onions
- crayons
- dental floss
- snails
- crabs

- slippers
- scabs
- coconuts
- straw
- chalk
- teddy bears
- pineapples
- salt and pepper
- curling irons

- earrings
- rocky road ice cream
- cavities
- bad hair days
- earlobes
- seashells
- babies
- paper clips
- squid

Generating Ideas: Idea Center

Background for the Teacher

Materials: thesaurus, baby name book, maps, dictionary, encyclopedia, calendars, magazines, newspapers, poetry collections, *Guinness Book of World Records*, and other reference materials; large box of crayons with the color names printed on the crayon wrapper; snapshots, postcards, travel brochures, and other visual materials; any other miscellaneous material that will stimulate students' imagination

Preparation: Place all materials into an area devoted to giving students ideas and references.

Lesson Presentation

Show students the idea center you have created. Explain to students how they can use each of the references in the center to generate topics for writing their poetry.

Depending on the materials you place in the center, your students may also find that some of the references help them to accurately revise their writing.

Skill Building: Using Rhyme

Background for the Teacher

Definition: Rhyme occurs when two or more words have the same sound.

Materials: reproductions of Nursery Rhymes worksheet (page 13)

Preparation: Reproduce one copy of the Nursery Rhymes worksheet for each group of students.

Lesson Plan

1. Place students in groups of four.

2. Assign each group one of the following words:

   - cat
   - door
   - ring
   - eat
   - man
   - shoe
   - pin

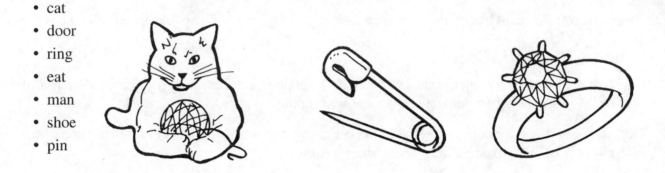

3. Instruct groups to list as many words that rhyme with their assigned word as possible in four minutes. Set a timer and instruct students to "Go!"

4. When time is up, have groups exchange papers with another group to be corrected and counted. You may wish to award a small prize such as a homework pass or stickers to the group with the most rhyming words or to all groups who followed directions correctly.

   Homework Pass

5. Review with students what it means when words rhyme.

6. Distribute Nursery Rhymes worksheet.

7. Working in their same groups, have students complete the nursery rhymes. Instruct students to pay particular attention to rhyming words as they complete the activity.

8. When students have completed the worksheet, direct students in a choral reading activity. All students in the class will read the nursery rhyme aloud at the same time. Hearing the rhyme through so many voices will reinforce for students the sound of the rhyme scheme in each nursery rhyme.

Nursery Rhymes

Directions: Complete the following nursery rhymes:

Humpty Dumpty sat on a wall.
Humpty Dumpty had a great _____.
All the King's horses and all the King's men
Couldn't put Humpty together _____

Mary had a little lamb
Its fleece was white as snow
And everywhere that Mary went
The lamb was sure to _____.

Jack and Jill
went up the _____
to fetch a pail of water.
Jack fell down
and broke his _____
and Jill came tumbling after!

Hey! diddle diddle!
The cat and the _____
The cow jumped over the moon;
The little dog laughed
To see such sport,
And the dish ran away with the _____.

Hinky-Pinky Rhymes

Background for the Teacher

Definition: A hinky-pinky is a pair of rhyming, two-syllable words. Similarly, a hink-pink and a hinkety-pinkety are rhyming pairs using one- and three-syllable words, respectively.

Skills Needed: counting syllables; rhyming

Materials: none

Preparation: none

Lesson Plan

Prewriting

1. Write the following riddle on the board:

   Question: What do you call it when it rains every day in June, July, and August?

   (**Answer:** a bummer summer)

2. Tell students that a rhyming riddle is called a hinky-pinky. Ask students how many syllables are in the words hinky and pinky. A hinky-pinky is when a pair of words that has two syllables rhymes; a hink-pink is a pair of one-syllable rhyming words; and a hinkety-pinkety is a pair of three-syllable rhyming words.

3. Generate one-, two-, and three-syllable rhyming pairs with students. Some possibilities include:

   - funny money
   - nice ice
   - fat cat
   - lucky ducky
   - beat feet
   - cool school
   - pest test

   - knot spot
   - bug hug
   - jelly belly
   - horse course
   - sloppy copy
   - sinister minister
   - double trouble

Drafting

1. Instruct students to choose 10 pairs of rhyming words from the class-generated list or from their own ideas.

2. Students are to draft question riddles to go with the rhyming pairs of words.

Hinky-Pinky Rhymes *(cont.)*

Revising/Editing

1. When students have completed the draft of 10 hinky-pinky rhymes (or hink-pinks or hinkety-pinketies), students should share their riddles with a peer responder. Provide the Hinky-Pinky Response and Assessment Sheet (page 17) for this purpose. Peer responders should check to ensure that each rhyming pair of words has the same number of syllables and that the riddles make sense.

2. Following peer response, students should make any necessary revisions before writing final copies of their riddles.

Publishing

Students could type their riddles using a word processing program and compile a class riddle book.

Student Samples of Hinky-Pinkies

- What do you call a clever insect? (*a sly fly*)

- What do you call humorous currency? (*funny money*)

- What did the fish say to the bait? (*"Squirm, worm!"*)

- What do you call a dead fire? (*lame flame*)

- What do you call a class clown? (*school fool*)

- What do you call an archeologist who studies pyramids and mummies? (*Tut nut*)

- What do you call the best police officer on the force? (*top cop*)

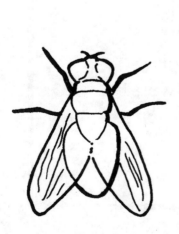

Content Connection for Hinky-Pinky Rhymes

Language Arts

Suppose your language arts teacher has asked you to write rhyming riddles using your vocabulary words. Before you write, think about which vocabulary words rhyme. Think about clever riddles for the pairs of words. Remember to make sure the riddle makes sense. Write hink-pink, hinky-pinky, or hinkety-pinkety riddles for your teacher using your rhyming vocabulary words.

Social Studies

Suppose your social studies teacher has asked you to write rhyming riddles about a period of history. Before you write, make up some hink-pinks that you can use as answers for riddles. Think about clever riddles that relate to the historical period that will fit with your hink-pink, hinky-pinky, or hinkety-pinkety answers. Remember to make sure the riddle makes sense. Share your riddles with the class.

Hinky-Pinky Response and Assessment Sheet

Author's Name _____

Poem Title _____

Responder's Name(s) _____ Date _____

Responder:

Did the author . . .

- ❏ write a question as the beginning of each riddle?
- ❏ include two rhyming words with the same number of syllables?
- ❏ write riddles that make sense?

Author:

Before writing your final copy, have you . . .

- ❏ made any necessary revisions from your peer response session?
- ❏ checked for proper spelling?
- ❏ checked for proper capitalization?
- ❏ checked for proper punctuation?

Revision suggestions: _____

Complete the following statements to provide some information about your writing:

I had a hard time _____.

My favorite part of writing hinky-pinky riddles is _____.

I would like to write another hinky-pinky sometime. (Circle one.)

Yes   No

Teacher:

_____ correct format of riddle

_____ appropriate word choice

_____ neatness

_____ correct spelling and mechanics

_____ _____

Score: _____

Skill Building: Using Rhythm

Background for the Teacher

Definition: Rhythm (or meter) is a regular pattern of accented and unaccented syllables in lines of poetry.

Materials: rhythm sticks or pencils (2 per student), a copy of a favorite poem that has a distinct rhythm

Preparation: Gather materials needed for lesson.

Lesson Plan

1. Clap your hands loudly in a rhythmic pattern to gain the attention of the class. Clap your hands again, using the same rhythm, and instruct students to answer by clapping the same rhythm.

2. Repeat this exercise several times.

3. Distribute rhythm sticks or pencils to pairs of students (each student will need two). Remind students to use rhythm sticks or pencils appropriately.

4. Instruct pairs to continue the same activity—one partner will establish a rhythm and tap it with pencils or rhythm sticks, the other partner will echo the pattern in answer.

5. After sufficient time, collect rhythm sticks or pencils from students.

6. In the same manner as the previous activity, recite a line from a poem, using inflection in your voice as you speak. Instruct students to repeat the same line, using the same inflection you used.

7. Continue with this exercise, instructing students to pay particular attention to the words you accent and don't accent. This pattern of accented and unaccented syllables is creating the rhythm of the line.

8. Finally, vocalize the rhythm in the first line of "There was an old woman who lived in a shoe" using only sound (e.g., "Da dá da da dá da da dá da da dá"). Instruct students to mimic the rhythm. Then, instruct students to compose a line of poetry, using any words they can, that has the same rhythm as this line of poetry. For example, they may write, "My mother can help me to water the plants."

9. Provide further practice in rhythm as needed.

Limerick

Background for the Teacher

Definition: A limerick is a five-line poem that is funny or nonsensical. The first line of the limerick often begins with "There once was . . . ." or "There was a . . . ." A limerick has a distinctive rhyme pattern, with lines 1, 2, and 5 rhyming together, and lines 3 and 4 rhyming together.

Skills Needed: understanding of rhyme and rhythm

Materials: Storytelling with Limericks worksheets (pages 21–23), Limerick Response and Assessment Sheets (page 26), markers, crayons, colored pencils

Preparation: Reproduce Storytelling with Limericks worksheets and Limerick Response and Assessment Sheets for each student in the class.

Lesson Plan

Prewriting

1. Have students close their eyes and think of a time that something funny happened to them or that they saw something funny happen to someone else.

2. Instruct students to turn to a partner and tell that student what the funny event was.

3. Distribute the Storytelling worksheets. Have students complete the first section about their funny event.

Drafting

1. Lead students through the remainder of the worksheet, writing the poem line by line based on the models provided. Encourage students to pay particular attention to the rhythm and rhyme scheme.

2. After the students have completed the five lines, have them rewrite their lines as a complete poem at the end of the worksheet.

Revising/Editing

1. When the poem is drafted, students should share their limericks with peer responders. Provide the Limerick Response and Assessment Sheet for this purpose. Peer responders should check to ensure that the correct rhythm and rhyme scheme have been used in each line.

2. Following peer response, students should make any necessary revisions before writing a final copy of the poem.

Publishing

Students could illustrate their final copy with a drawing of the funny event being described in the limerick.

Student Samples of Limericks

There once was a man on the moon
Who flew in a hot air balloon.
To the red planet Mars,
Where he sold brand new cars
For Martians to ride on the dunes.

There was a young girl from Tibet
Who couldn't pay off all her debt
She bet on a horse—
Real money, of course—
It's lucky she won the big bet.

There once was a mighty big dog
Who thought he was really a frog.
He would leap in the air
And people would stare,
He'd land perfectly upon a fat log.

There once was a nice girl from France
Who knew how to sing and to dance.
Each day she danced more,
Her feet got so sore,
She danced herself into a trance.

Storytelling with Limericks

Think of the funny event you shared with your partner during class discussion. Answer the following questions about your funny event:

Who was involved?

_____

Where did it take place?

_____

What happened?

_____

How did it end?

_____

Writing Line 1

Write a limerick about this event. A limerick is a poem that tells a story. Use one of the two beginnings below to start your limerick. Write only one line right now. Tell *who* was involved in the event and *where* it happened.

Choose and complete one of the classic openings for a limerick:

There once was a (n)

_____

or

There was a (n)

_____

The line you just wrote will become the first line of your limerick. Limericks tell a funny or nonsense story and follow a certain rhyme scheme and rhythm pattern.

Storytelling with Limericks *(cont.)*

Writing Line 1 *(cont.)*

Listen to the rhythm of the first lines to several limericks:

There once was a man on the moon . . .

There was a young girl from Tibet . . .

The lines have the same rhythm, don't they?

Now, revise the first line that you wrote earlier so that its rhythm sounds like the sample lines above. Listen carefully to the accented and unaccented words. Your line should match the rhythm of the others very closely.

Write your revised first line here:

_____

Go back to the line you just wrote and circle the last word. This will be an important word to remember when you write your second line.

Writing Line 2

The second line of a limerick has the exact same rhythm as the first line. It tells a little more information about the person in the first line. Notice, too, that the last word in the first line and the last word in the second line rhyme.

> There once was a man on the *moon*
>
> Who flew in a hot air *balloon* . . .

> There once was a girl from *Tibet*
>
> Who couldn't pay off all her *debt* . . .

Now, write a second line for your limerick, telling a little more information about the person in the limerick. Remember, make your first and second lines have the same rhythm. Be sure that the last words in each line rhythm.

Write your second line here:

_____

Writing Lines 3 and 4

The third and fourth lines of a limerick have a different rhythm and a slightly different rhyme scheme than the first two lines. They tell what happened in the funny story. Here is an example of a third and fourth line. Notice the rhythm and rhyme.

> There once was a girl from Tibet
>
> Who couldn't pay off all her debt.
>
> She bet on a *horse*—
>
> Real money, of *course*—

Now, write your third and fourth lines here:

_____

_____

Storytelling with Limericks *(cont.)*

Writing Line 5

The last line of a limerick has the same rhyme scheme and rhythm as the first two lines. Here is an example of a final line:

> There once was a girl from *Tibet*
> Who couldn't pay off all her *debt*.
> She bet on a horse—
> Real money, of course—
> It's lucky she won the big *bet*!

Write your last line here. Make sure the last word rhymes with the last words in lines 1 and 2.

_____

Congratulations! You have completed a limerick! Now, rewrite each line in poem form so that it is easier to read.

Content Connections for Limericks

Science

Suppose your science teacher has asked you to describe the sequence of a scientific process that you have been studying. Your teacher would like you to write your sequence in limerick form. Think about what happens in the beginning of the sequence, what happens in the middle, and what happens at the end of the sequence. Be sure to keep your description short since a limerick is only five lines long! Write a limerick describing the sequence of a scientific process you have been studying.

Fine Arts

Suppose your fine arts teacher has asked you to describe the events illustrated in a work of art you are studying. Your teacher would like you to write your description of events in limerick form. Think about what is happening in the illustration. Think about what might have occurred first, what might have occurred next, and what might have occurred last. Write a limerick describing the events illustrated in a work of art you are studying.

Content Connections for Limericks *(cont.)*

Language Arts

Suppose your language arts teacher has asked you to review the plot of a story you have just read. Your teacher would like you to write your summary in limerick form. Think about what happened in the beginning of the story, what happened in the middle of the story, and what happened at the end of the story. Be sure to keep your summary short since a limerick is only five lines long! Write a limerick summarizing the plot of the story you have just read.

Social Studies

Suppose your social studies teacher has asked you to retell a sequence of historical events you have been studying. Your teacher would like you to write your sequence in limerick form. Think about the order in which the historical events occurred. Be sure to keep your sequence short since a limerick is only five lines long! Write a limerick retelling the sequence of historical events you have been studying.

Limerick Response and Assessment Sheet

Author's Name _____

Poem Title _____

Responder's Name(s) _____ Date: _____

Responder:

Did the author . . .

❑ maintain the correct rhythm for each line?

❑ rhyme lines 1, 2, and 5?

❑ rhyme lines 3 and 4?

❑ tell a funny story?

❑ use the best possible word choice?

Revision suggestions: _____

_____

Author:

Before writing your final copy, have you . . .

❑ made any necessary revisions from your peer response session?

❑ checked for proper spelling?

❑ checked for proper capitalization?

❑ checked for proper punctuation?

Complete the following statements to provide some information about your writing:

I had a hard time _____.

My favorite part of the poem is _____.

I would like to write another limerick sometime. (Circle one.)

Yes   No

Teacher:

_____ correct format of poem

_____ appropriate word choice

_____ neatness

_____ correct spelling and mechanics

_____ _____

Score: _____

Skill Building: Using Alliteration

Background for the Teacher

Definition: Alliteration is the repetition of the same beginning consonant or vowel sounds in words.

Materials: reproduction of Alliteration Action worksheet (page 28); highlighters, colored pencils, or markers for each student

Preparation: Reproduce Alliteration Action worksheet for each student.

Lesson Plan

1. Write the following tongue twisters on the chalkboard or overhead projector:

   Betty bought a batch of buns at the bakery.

   Sammy swam, and sat, and sang, all by the seashore.

   Large Larry Lewis lounges at the lake.

2. Call on several students to try to say the tongue twisters as quickly as they can. Let students have fun with this! Ask students what makes tongue twisters so difficult to say. Hopefully, they will recognize that the repetition of the same consonant sound makes it difficult to pronounce the words quickly.

3. Define alliteration for students. Point out the alliteration in each of the tongue twisters from #1.

4. Explain that alliteration is a technique poets sometimes use to make their poems catchy or interesting to the reader.

5. Distribute the Alliteration Action worksheet. Two more tongue twisters are provided for students to try to pronounce in the first section of the worksheet. Using a highlighter, colored pencil, or markers, students can highlight the initial consonant sound in each of the words of the tongue twisters.

6. Allow students to complete the second section of the worksheet independently, underlining the alliterative consonants in the three examples provided.

7. Depending on the skill level of your students, they can complete the third section of alliterative lines independently or with partners. Check their completed lines for accuracy.

8. Provide extra practice in alliteration, as needed.

Alliteration Action

Alliteration is a technique in which the beginning consonant or vowel sounds are repeated in words for effect. Tongue twisters often use alliteration to make the phrases catchy. Notice the effect of alliteration as you try to say the following tongue twisters:

> Six silly sailors swam south.
>
> Bobby bought a bunch of brown bananas.

Alliteration Practice

Directions: Underline the alliterative consonants in these lines.

Example: Snakes slither on the sidewalk.

1. The wind whistled through the willows.

2. Magic markers can make masterpieces.

3. Tommy tried to twist, but tumbled.

Directions: Finish these lines using additional alliteration.

1. People patiently _____

   _____.

2. Roger ran _____

   _____.

3. Six swimmers_____

   _____.

4. Allen always _____

   _____.

5. Dona drove_____

   _____.

6. Gorgeous, gentle _____

   _____.

7. Jam jiggled_____

   _____.

8. Little Lotte _____

   _____.

Tongue Twister Poem

Background for the Teacher

Definition: A tongue twister poem uses alliteration to create tongue twisters that form the lines of the poem.

Skills Needed: understanding of alliteration and rhyme

Materials: reproductions of Amazing Animal Actions worksheet (page 32), Animal Tongue Twister Poem (page 33), and Tongue Twister Poem Response and Assessment Sheet (page 35); foam meat trays for each student; black construction paper cut into ½" x 4" or 5" (1.2 cm x 10 or 13 cm) strips (The size of the strips will depend on the size of your meat tray); magazine photos of animals or animal stickers; yarn; tape or glue

Preparation: Reproduce an Amazing Animal Actions worksheet and Tongue Twister Poem Response and Assessment Sheet for each student. Cut black construction paper into ½" x 4" or 5".

Lesson Plan

Prewriting

1. Have students complete the following lines using alliteration.

   The tiger tied up traffic with his _____.

   Snakes slithered slowly _____.

2. Read a student sample of a tongue twister poem.

3. Explain to students that the poem is somewhat silly because of the alliteration the author has used in the poem. Alliteration can make a silly topic such as eating food the wrong way sound even sillier.

4. Tell students that you will be showing them how to write a tongue twister poem about a funny day at the zoo.

5. Distribute Amazing Animal Actions worksheet. Have students list names of different animals on the chart provided. Suggest that students use animals that begin with different letters so that it is not too difficult to find alliterative words.

6. Work through the activity with students by modeling on the overhead or chalkboard. For each animal listed, brainstorm an action, a location, and more description using alliteration. A completed example has been provided for student reference.

Tongue Twister Poem *(cont.)*

Drafting

1. When students have completed the Amazing Animal Actions worksheet and are satisfied with their alliteration, distribute the Animal Tongue Twister Poem worksheet (page 33).

2. Read the first two lines and the last four lines with the students. Instruct them to use their animal alliteration to fill in the lines in the middle. Point out the rhyme pattern at the beginning and end. Encourage students to use the same couplet pattern when adding their alliterations. (They could use the goat example to provide an even number of animal lines.)

3. When their poem is complete, they should have a poem about the crazy animal mishaps at the zoo that day.

Revising/Editing

1. When the poem is drafted, students should share their tongue twister poems with peer responders. Provide the Tongue Twister Poem Response and Assessment Sheet (page 35) for this purpose. Peer responders should check to make sure that each line describes the antics of a different animal and that several alliterative words are used in each line.

2. Following peer response, students should make any necessary revisions before writing a final copy of the poem.

Publishing

1. Each student's poem could be combined in a class display of tongue twister poems. Distribute one foam meat tray to each student in the class.

2. Have the students glue or tape the final copies of their poems to the insides of the meat trays.

3. Students could decorate the inside of the trays with stickers or pictures of their animals.

4. Over the top of the poem and attached to the top and bottom edges of the meat tray, students can glue or tape "cages" made out of black construction paper strips.

5. Each animal cage could be connected with yarn and mounted to the wall as a class display of animal cages at the zoo.

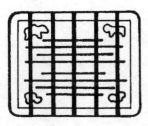 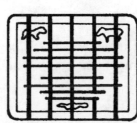 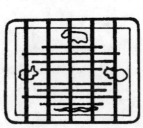 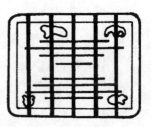

Student Samples of Tongue Twister Poems

You wouldn't believe the way my day started
It seemed my good manners with food had departed!
The toast wouldn't toast, no matter how hard I tried,
The bacon refused to budge or be fried.
My marmalade muffin was mushed on my mouth,
The sausage it sailed off my fork, heading south.
My jittery hands dropped the juice—the whole jug!
Scrambled in my eggs—a slimy stink bug!
Despite the bad start, my day was okay,
That is, until lunch—it went on the same way!

Silly Sam Smith slinks through the store
Trying on clothes 'til he can't try anymore.
A hat on his head, a hockey mask, too
Socks and shoes, more and more till he's blue!
Jeans, shorts, and shirts—
He even tries skirts!
Why, you ask, does Sam do these things?
He wants to be sure before the register rings
That the clothes will look great—
Kind of silly, since Sam Smith's only eight!

My friends and I went shopping.
Here is what we got:
Annie ate the apples as she shopped.
Betty bought a batch of fresh baked biscuits.
Carol cornered candy, cakes, and cucumbers.
Danny danced in delight with the fresh-dipped donuts.
Evan even entered the express lane.
Freddie found the franks and frozen French fries.
Gunther got green grapes and grated cheese.
Haley had her hands on a huge ham.
Igor idled up to the ice cream.
Justin jumped up high to reach the juice.
Kim kept the king-sized chips.
Luckily for us, my name is Lisa.
I'm the last to shop, and I apologized for my loony friends!

Amazing Animal Actions

Animal	Does What?	Where?	Why, How, or When?
A goat	greets guests	at the grocery store	wearing a green girdle
_____	_____	_____	_____
_____	_____	_____	_____
_____	_____	_____	_____
_____	_____	_____	_____
_____	_____	_____	_____
_____	_____	_____	_____
_____	_____	_____	_____
_____	_____	_____	_____
_____	_____	_____	_____
_____	_____	_____	_____
_____	_____	_____	_____
_____	_____	_____	_____
_____	_____	_____	_____
_____	_____	_____	_____
_____	_____	_____	_____

Animal Tongue Twister Poem

Something happened at the zoo today!

The animals got free and ran away!

_____

_____

_____

_____

_____

_____

I never heard of such commotion!

I hope the zookeeper has a magic potion

To get all the animals where they belong

Without anymore mishaps or things going wrong!

Written by _____

Content Connections for Tongue Twister Poems

Science

Suppose your science teacher has asked you to describe the characteristics of an animal you are studying. Your teacher would like you to write your description as a tongue twister poem. Think about an animal you are studying. Think about what the animal looks like, where it lives, what it eats, and other important facts. Write a tongue twister poem describing the characteristics of an animal you are studying.

Social Studies

Suppose your social studies teacher has asked you to retell a sequence of historical events you have been studying. Your teacher would like you to write your sequence as a tongue twister poem. Think about the order in which the historical events occurred. Think about how you could make the events funny or humorous since you are writing them as a tongue twister. Write a tongue twister poem retelling the sequence of historical events you have been studying.

Tongue Twister Poem Response and Assessment Sheet

Author's Name _____

Poem Title _____

Responder's Name(s) _____ Date _____

Responder:

Did the author . . .

- ❏ write about a different animal on each line?
- ❏ use several alliterative words in each line?
- ❏ maintain the established rhyme scheme?
- ❏ use the best possible word choice?

Revision suggestions: _____

_____

Author:

Before writing your final copy, have you . . .

- ❏ made any necessary revisions from your peer response session?
- ❏ checked for proper spelling?
- ❏ checked for proper capitalization?
- ❏ checked for proper punctuation?

Complete the following statements to provide some information about your writing:

I had a hard time _____.

My favorite part of the poem is _____.

I would like to write another tongue twister poem sometime. (Circle one.)

                    Yes   No

Teacher:

_____ correct format of poem

_____ appropriate word choice

_____ neatness

_____ correct spelling and mechanics

_____ _____

Score: _____

© Teacher Created Resources, Inc.   35   #2992 Poetry Writing—Grades 3–5

Skill Building: Counting Syllables

Background for the Teacher

Definition: Syllables are the divisions of sounds in words.

Materials: highlighters, colored pencils, or markers; reproductions of Counting Sounds worksheet (page 38)

Preparation: Reproduce Counting Sounds worksheet for each student in the class. Gather other materials needed for lesson.

Lesson Plan

1. Write the following words on the chalkboard or overhead projector:

• cat	• gorilla	• alligator
• monkey	• elephant	• snake

2. Explain to students that syllables are the way words are divided when they are pronounced.

3. Count with students the number of syllables in each of the words from #1. Demonstrate how to clap the syllables as they are pronounced. Some students like to count the syllables by placing a hand under the chin and counting the number of times the chin drops. You may wish to demonstrate this method as well. After the number of syllables is identified for each word, have students use their colored highlighters, pencils, or crayons to underline each syllable in the word. Each syllable should be underlined, using a different color to provide a visual reference for students.

Word	Syllable(s)
cat	(1)
monkey	(2)
gorilla	(3)
elephant	(3)
alligator	(4)
snake	(1)

4. Ask students to think of words with a certain number of syllables. Divide students into groups of three or four students. Instruct each group to write one word that has one syllable, one word that has two syllables, one word that has three syllables, and one word that has four syllables.

Skill Building: Counting Syllables *(cont.)*

Lesson Plan *(cont.)*

5. Invite students to share the group-generated words with the class, checking for accuracy as the words are shared.

6. Explain to students that sometimes, whole lines of words are counted for their syllables. Ask students to count the syllables in the following lines:

   Red and brown leaves fall   (5)

   In a forest all alone   (7)

   Blanketing the ground   (5)

7. Working in the same groups, instruct students to write a line of words that has five syllables in it.

8. Check for accuracy by having groups share their lines with the class.

9. Distribute the Counting Syllables worksheet. Review the directions with students before they complete the sheet independently.

10. Assess student understanding by reviewing the worksheet after it is completed and providing extra practice for students as needed.

Counting Sounds

A syllable is a unit of sound that makes a beat when pronounced in a word. Some people like to clap out syllables. Some people place a hand under the chin and count each time the chin goes down when saying a word. Practice counting the syllables in the following words:

lazy _____   amazing _____   mine _____

police _____   dictionary _____   second _____

century _____   captured _____   ambulance _____

Now try writing a word that has the following number of syllables:

(2) _____

(3) _____

(1) _____

(5) _____

Try writing whole lines that have a certain number of syllables. For example, the following line has five syllables in it:

(5) Trees stand tall and proud.

Now you try it! Write a line that contains the same number of syllables as the number in parentheses.

(5) _____

(7) _____

(4) _____

(6) _____

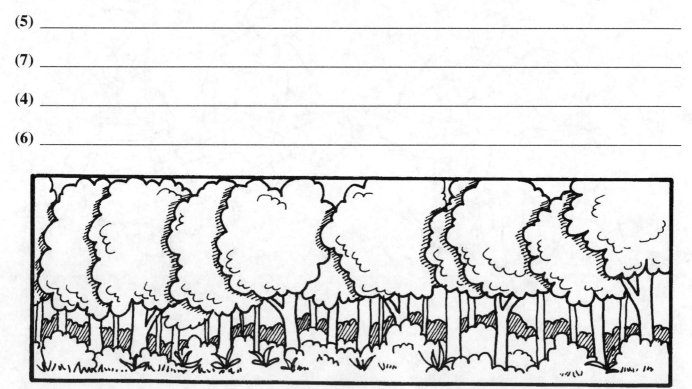

Standards and Benchmarks: 1A, 1B, 1C, 2A, 3D, 3E, 3F, 3J

Haiku

Background for the Teacher

Definition: Haiku is an unrhymed, three-line poem. The first line has five syllables, the second line has seven syllables, and the third line has five syllables. The subject of a haiku is usually something beautiful in nature.

Skills Needed: counting syllables

Materials: laminated calendar photographs depicting beautiful nature scenes, reproductions of Haiku Response and Assessment Sheet (page 43), watercolors or other media for illustrating final copies of poems

Preparation: Collect pictures from calendars depicting scenes in nature. Laminate pictures for durability. Reproduce a Haiku Response and Assessment Sheet for each student in the class.

Lesson Plan

Prewriting

1. Explain to students that they will be writing a haiku. Haiku is an ancient form of Japanese poetry that follows a particular pattern of syllables in its lines. The topic of a haiku is most often something beautiful in nature.

2. Distribute calendar photographs to students. Ask them to study their pictures closely for one minute.

3. After one minute, have students turn to a partner and describe their pictures to their partners. As one partner describes a picture, the other partner should record in writing what that person is saying. This will be given back to the partner describing the picture to serve as a written record of the student's initial ideas. Allow enough time to complete this activity for both partners' pictures.

Drafting

1. Share several student samples of haiku. Count the syllables in each line with the students. Note the precise word choice authors have used since there is no room for extra words in the haiku syllable pattern.

2. Instruct students to draft haikus about their calendar pictures. They may refer to their partner's written record of their description for ideas. Remind them of the 5-7-5 syllable pattern for haiku.

Revising/Editing

1. When the poem is drafted, students should share their haikus with peer responders. Provide the Haiku Response and Assessment Sheet for this purpose. Peer responders should check to make sure that each line has the correct number of syllables and that strong, descriptive words have been used.

2. Following peer response, students should make any necessary revisions before writing a final copy of the poem.

Haiku *(cont.)*

Publishing

Since haikus are often about something beautiful in nature, students may wish to illustrate their haikus with pictures depicting the scenes in their poems. Watercolors, with their soft effect, complement haikus well. Pastels and charcoals are other possibilities; spray pictures with hair spray or lacquer in a well-ventilated area to keep the artwork from smearing.

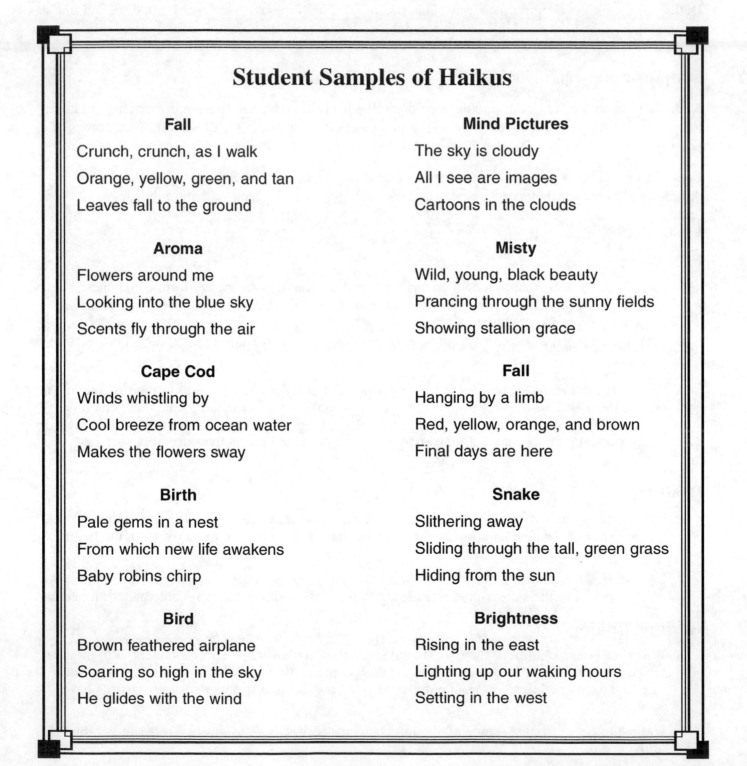

Student Samples of Haikus

Fall

Crunch, crunch, as I walk

Orange, yellow, green, and tan

Leaves fall to the ground

Aroma

Flowers around me

Looking into the blue sky

Scents fly through the air

Cape Cod

Winds whistling by

Cool breeze from ocean water

Makes the flowers sway

Birth

Pale gems in a nest

From which new life awakens

Baby robins chirp

Bird

Brown feathered airplane

Soaring so high in the sky

He glides with the wind

Mind Pictures

The sky is cloudy

All I see are images

Cartoons in the clouds

Misty

Wild, young, black beauty

Prancing through the sunny fields

Showing stallion grace

Fall

Hanging by a limb

Red, yellow, orange, and brown

Final days are here

Snake

Slithering away

Sliding through the tall, green grass

Hiding from the sun

Brightness

Rising in the east

Lighting up our waking hours

Setting in the west

Content Connections for Haikus

Science

Suppose your science teacher has asked you to describe the appearance of a plant or animal you are studying. Your teacher would like you to write your description as a haiku. Think about a plant or animal you are studying. Think about the shape, color, and size of the plant or animal. Think about any unique characteristics of the plant or animal's appearance. Write a haiku describing the appearance of a plant or animal you are studying.

Social Studies

Suppose your social studies teacher has asked you to describe a geographical region or landmark you have been studying. Your teacher would like you to write your description as a haiku poem. Think about the region or landmark you have been studying. Think about where it is located, what size it is, what shape it is, and what color(s) it is. Write a haiku describing a geographical region or landmark you have been studying.

Content Connections
for Haikus *(cont.)*

Language Arts

Suppose your language arts teacher has asked you to describe a scene in a story you have been reading. Your teacher would like you to write your description as a haiku poem. Think about a scene in the story. Think about the setting and time of the scene. Think about specific features such as buildings or parks that may be in the scene. Write a haiku describing a scene in a story you have been reading.

Fine Arts

Suppose your fine arts teacher has asked you to record your impression of a work of art you have been studying. This may be a painting, a sculpture, or a musical composition. Your teacher would like you to write your impression as a haiku poem.

Think about the work of art you have been studying. Think about how it makes you feel. Think about any images the art brings to mind. Think about the colors, shapes, or sounds that were used to create the art. Write a haiku recording your impression of a work of art you have been studying.

Haiku Response and Assessment Sheet

Author's Name _____

Poem Title_____

Responder's Name(s) _____ Date _____

Responder:

Did the author . . .

- ❑ include 5 syllables in the first line?
- ❑ include 7 syllables in the second line?
- ❑ include 5 syllables in the third line?
- ❑ write about something beautiful in nature?
- ❑ use the best possible word choice?

Revision suggestions: _____

_____

Author:

Before writing your final copy, have you . . .

- ❑ made any necessary revisions from your peer response session?
- ❑ checked for proper spelling?
- ❑ checked for proper capitalization?
- ❑ checked for proper punctuation?

Complete the following statements to provide some information about your writing:

I had a hard time _____.

My favorite part of the poem is _____.

I would like to write another haiku sometime. (Circle one.)

                       Yes   No

Teacher:

_____ correct format of poem

_____ appropriate word choice

_____ neatness

_____ correct spelling and mechanics

_____ _____

Score: _____

Lowku

Background for the Teacher

Definition: Lowku is an unrhymed, three-line poem. The first line has five syllables, the second line has seven syllables, and the third line has five syllables. The subject of a lowku is usually something disgusting in everyday life.

Skills Needed: counting syllables

Materials: Lowku Response and Assessment Sheet (page 47), scraps of construction paper, glue or tape

Preparation: Gather materials needed for lesson.

Lesson Plan

Prewriting

1. Have students brainstorm a list of things they think are gross and disgusting. You may wish to make a class list of "approved" disgusting things since student enthusiasm can sometimes lead the topics to get out of hand. Here are some suggestions:

   - trash
   - banana peels
   - fingernail parings
   - smog
   - leftovers
   - cigarette butts
   - snail trails
   - grease

2. Explain to students that they will be writing a lowku poem. Lowku is similar to haiku since it has the same syllable pattern. However, the subject of a lowku is not something beautiful, but rather something disgusting or "low."

Drafting

1. Instruct students to select one of the disgusting topics from the class list. This will be the subject of their lowkus.

2. Following the structure of the haiku (5–7–5 syllable pattern), direct students to write a lowku about their disgusting topic.

Revising/Editing

1. When the poems are drafted, students should share their lowkus with peer responders. Provide the Lowku Response and Assessment Sheet for this purpose. Peer responders should check to make sure that each line has the correct number of syllables and that strong, descriptive words have been used.

2. Following peer response, students should make any necessary revisions before writing a final copy of the poems.

Publishing

Students could use scraps of paper to create an "ugly color" collage. The collage could be used as a frame for the lowku.

Student Samples of Lowku

Mud

I step in the mud
I track the mud in my house
Mom yells to clean up

Slime

I pick up the rock
Worms are sliding all around
I drop the rock. Gross!

Bags

Looking in the trash
For my morning breakfast dish
It's life on the streets

P-U!

Shoes and socks are off
The stink soon floats through the air
I will hold my nose

Sniffles

You need a tissue
Blow your runny nose on it
Throw it in the trash

Smog

In the city air
Gray clouds fill the sky above
No one dares to breathe

Sluggish

Lazy like a slug
I just want to sleep today
Roll over and snore

Trash

Floating in the lake
Why don't people throw it out?
Polluting my world

Content Connections for Lowku

Science

Suppose your science teacher has asked you to describe your feelings about a particular environmental problem that you are studying. Your teacher would like you to write your description as a lowku. Think about how the environmental problem affects people. Think about how you feel about this problem. Write a lowku describing your feelings about a particular environmental problem you are studying.

Social Studies

Suppose your social studies teacher has asked you to describe your feelings about a war you have been studying. Your teacher would like you to write your description as a lowku. Think about a war you have been studying. Think about what caused the war. Think about what happened during the war. Think about how studying the war makes you feel. Write a lowku describing your feelings about a war you have been studying.

Lowku Response and Assessment Sheet

Author's Name _____

Poem Title _____

Responder's Name(s) _____ Date _____

Responder:

Did the author . . .

- ❏ include 5 syllables in the first line?
- ❏ include 7 syllables in the second line?
- ❏ include 5 syllables in the third line?
- ❏ write about something disgusting?
- ❏ use the best possible word choice?

Revision suggestions: _____

_____

Author:

Before writing your final copy, have you . . .

- ❏ made any necessary revisions from your peer response session?
- ❏ checked for proper spelling?
- ❏ checked for proper capitalization?
- ❏ checked for proper punctuation?

Complete the following statements to provide some information about your writing:

I had a hard time _____.

My favorite part of the poem is _____.

I would like to write another lowku sometime. (Circle one.)

Yes   No

Teacher:

_____ correct format of poem

_____ appropriate word choice

_____ neatness

_____ correct spelling and mechanics

_____ _____

Score: _____

Diamante

Background for the Teacher

Definition: A diamante is a poem written in the shape of a diamond. The form begins with a short line, its lines become progressively longer, and then its lines become shorter again. The diamante has several pattern variations. This lesson will teach students how to write a diamante using two opposite topics.

Skills Needed: familiarity with the basic parts of speech (nouns, adjectives, verbs)

Materials: one diamond cutout from the reproducible Diamante Diamonds (page 51) for each student, one Absolutely Opposites worksheet (page 52) for each pair of students, one Diamante Response and Assessment Sheet (page 56) for each pair of students, envelope or plastic sandwich bag, Diamond Design pattern (page 53) for students to trace, construction paper or aluminum foil

Preparation: Cut out the diamonds on the Diamante Diamonds reproducible. Store diamonds in an envelope or plastic sandwich bag until needed for the lesson. Reproduce the Absolutely Opposites worksheet and the Diamante Response and Assessment Sheet. Reproduce and cut out a Diamond Design pattern for each student in the class.

Lesson Plan

Prewriting

1. Distribute one diamond cutout to each student at the beginning of class. Instruct students to read the word on their diamond and locate the student who has the diamond with the opposite of their diamond word. Allow students time to move around the room to locate their "opposite partner." Once students have located their partner, instruct them to sit together. They will be writing partners for this lesson.

2. Distribute the Absolutely Opposites worksheet. Instruct students to write one of the words from their diamonds in the box marked Opposite #1. The opposite word from the other diamond should be written in the box marked Opposite #2.

3. Instruct students to complete the worksheet, following the directions in the boxes. Depending on the skill level of your students, you may need to review adjectives, verbs, and nouns.

Diamante *(cont.)*

Drafting

1. Once students have generated the content for their diamante, instruct them to draft the poem in diamond form. The poem should be written in the following pattern:

   Line 1   Opposite #1

   Line 2   2 adjectives describing Opposite #1

   Line 3   3 verbs related to Opposite #1

   Line 4   2 nouns related to Opposite #1; 2 nouns related to Opposite #2

   Line 5   3 verbs related to Opposite #2

   Line 6   2 adjectives describing Opposite #2

   Line 7   Opposite #2

Revising/Editing

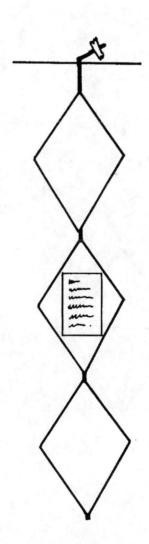

1. When the poem is drafted, students should share their diamante with another pair of students. Provide the Diamante Response and Assessment Sheet for this purpose. Peer responders should check to make sure the correct format has been followed, including the number of words and parts of speech. Students should also make sure that the poem resembles a diamond shape.

2. Following peer response, students should make any necessary revisions before writing a final copy of the poem.

Publishing

Students could write their diamante on a piece of white paper and mount it on a piece of construction paper or aluminum foil cut in the shape of a large diamond; the Diamond Design could be used by students to trace the shape of a diamond. They could attach the poem to two other diamonds illustrating the opposites they wrote about in their poem. The finished product is a string of three diamonds connected together, with the poem in the middle. These look wonderful hanging from the ceiling or walls as a classroom display. (Be sure to check on your school or district policy on hanging items from the ceiling before doing so.)

Student Samples of Diamantes

tropical

warm, summery

swimming, sunning, surfing

sandy beaches, hula girls, polar bears, Santa Claus

freezing, snowing, blowing

cold, wintry

Arctic

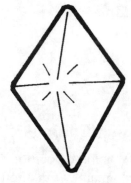

sad

lonely, weepy

crying, wishing, missing

hurt, tears, smile, joy

laughing, clapping, leaping

excited, cheery

glad

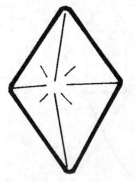

hot

steamy, humid

burning, sizzling, cooking

fire, heat, ice, snow

blowing, biting, freezing

frigid, chilly

cold

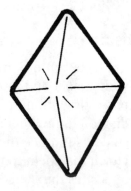

Diamante Diamonds

Follow the directions on page 48.

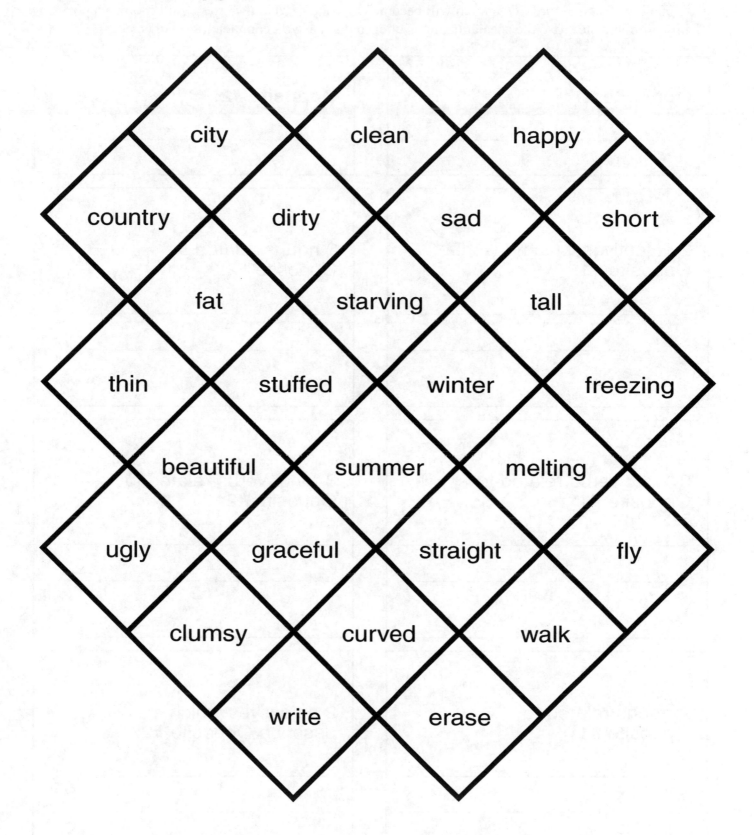

Absolutely Opposites

Think of two nouns that are significantly opposite from one another, such as winter and summer, old and young, or fish and bird. One noun will become Opposite #1, and the other will become Opposite #2 in your diamante. Use the special qualities of each noun as you complete this worksheet.

Opposite #1:

_____

Opposite #2:

_____

2 adjectives which describe Opposite #1:

_____

_____

2 nouns related to Opposite #2:

_____

_____

3 "-ing" verbs related to Opposite #1:

_____

_____

3 "-ing" verbs related to Opposite #2:

_____

_____

2 nouns related to Opposite #1:

_____

_____

2 adjectives which describe Opposite #2:

_____

_____

Diamond Design

Use the template below for writing your diamante.

Content Connections for Diamantes

Language Arts

Suppose your language arts teacher has asked you to compare two very different characters from a story you have been reading. Your teacher would like you to write your comparison as a diamante poem. Think about two different characters from a story you have been reading. Think about their appearances. Think about their personalities. Think about their actions. Think about how the characters are different. Write a diamante comparing two different characters from a story you have been reading.

Math

Suppose your math teacher has asked you to compare two geometric shapes. Your teacher would like you to write your comparison as a diamante poem. Think about two geometric shapes. Think about their appearances. Think about real objects that are designed in the two shapes you have chosen. Think about how the shapes are different. Write a diamante comparing two different geometric shapes.

Content Connections for Diamantes *(cont.)*

Social Studies

Suppose your social studies teacher has asked you to compare two opposite concepts, such as freedom and slavery or peace and war. Your teacher would like you to write your comparison as a diamante poem. Think about the two different concepts your teacher has assigned. Think about the definitions of the concepts. Think about examples of the concepts. Think about society's feelings toward the concepts. Write a diamante comparing the two opposite concepts assigned by your teacher.

Science

Suppose your science teacher has asked you to compare two planets. Your teacher would like you to write your comparison as a diamante poem. Think about two planets you have been studying. Think about their appearances. Think about their locations. Think about the environments and atmospheres of the planets. Write a diamante comparing two planets that you have been studying.

Fine Arts

Suppose your fine arts teacher has asked you to compare two different styles of art or music. Your teacher would like you to write your comparison as a diamante poem. Think about the two different styles. Think about the time period in which each style was prominent. Think about what the style looks or sounds like. Think about specific artists who used each style. Write a diamante comparing the two styles of art or music assigned by your teacher.

Diamante Response and Assessment Sheet

Author's Name _____

Poem Title _____

Responder's Name(s) _____ Date _____

Responder:

Did the author . . .

❑ use the correct number of words on each line?

❑ use the correct part of speech on each line?

❑ include only words related to the topic?

❑ use the best possible word choice?

Revision suggestions: _____

_____

Author:

Before writing your final copy, have you . . .

❑ made any necessary revisions from your peer response session?

❑ checked for proper spelling?

❑ checked for proper capitalization?

❑ checked for proper punctuation?

Complete the following statements to provide some information about your writing:

I had a hard time _____.

My favorite part of the poem is _____.

I would like to write another diamante sometime. (Circle one.)

              Yes   No

Teacher:

_____ correct format of poem

_____ appropriate word choice

_____ neatness

_____ correct spelling and mechanics

_____ _____

Score: _____

Cinquain

Background for the Teacher

Definition: A cinquain is a poem that is written following a specific formula: The first line of a cinquain is a noun that is the topic of the poem, the second line contains two adjectives that describe the noun, the third line contains three verbs that show actions that the noun performs, the fourth line contains a four-word phrase about the noun, and the last line repeats the noun again or uses a synonym of the noun.

Skills Needed: understanding of parts of speech (noun, verb, adjective)

Materials: reproductions of Cinquain on the Brain (page 59) for each student and Student Samples of Cinquains (page 58) for each pair of students, construction paper, scissors, glue or tape

Preparation: Reproduce Cinquain on the Brain worksheet and Student Samples of Cinquains. Gather other materials needed for the lesson.

Lesson Plan

Prewriting

1. Brainstorm a list of nouns on the chalkboard.

2. Ask students to select one noun to use as the topic of their cinquains.

3. Distribute the Cinquain on the Brain worksheet. Review the directions with the students. Depending on the skill level of your students, you may need to review basic parts of speech before instructing them to complete the worksheet.

4. Provide students with the student samples of cinquains. Instruct students to work with a partner to deduce the pattern for cinquain poems.

5. When students think they have determined the formula for the poem, have students share their thoughts with the class. Write the pattern for a cinquain on the board:

   Line 1: noun

   Line 2: two adjectives describing the noun

   Line 3: three verbs showing the actions of the noun

   Line 4: a four-word phrase telling about the noun

   Line 5: repetition of the noun or use of a synonym for the noun

Cinquain Poem *(cont.)*

Drafting

Instruct students to use the formula to draft a cinquain about their topic.

Revising/Editing

1. When the poem is drafted, students should share their cinquain with another student. Provide the Cinquain Response and Assessment Sheet for this purpose. Peer responders should check to make sure that the correct part of speech is included on each line, that the correct number of words is used on each line, and that the overall poem makes sense.

2. Following peer response, students should make any necessary revisions before writing a final copy of the poem.

Publishing

1. Have students each cut out a shape of their object from construction paper that is larger than the copy of their poem so that it can be used as a frame.

2. Instruct students to mount their final copy of the poem on the outline shape of their object. The final product could be hung from the ceiling as a mobile for an attractive classroom display. (Be sure to check your school or district policy regarding hanging items from the ceiling before doing so.)

Student Samples of Cinquains

Dirt
Sloppy, muddy
Covering, fertilizing, splattering
Pigs roll in it
Dirt

Sneakers
White, squeaky
Running, jumping, skipping
They cover my feet
Nike

Ocean
Salty, wet
Rolling, crashing, spraying
Habitat for sea animals
Water

Star
Bright, shiny
Twinkling, gleaming, sparkling
Make wishes come true
Star

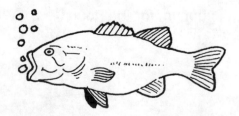

Cinquain on the Brain

Write the topic of your poem here. Remember, it should be a noun.

Example: cloud

_____   _____

_____   _____

Write several adjectives to describe your topic on the lines below.

Examples: fluffy, white, soft, circular

_____   _____

_____   _____

Write several actions that your noun performs on the lines below.

Examples: floats, glides, covers the sky, sails through the sky

_____   _____

_____   _____

Write some phrases about your topic here.

Examples: cumulus are my favorite

_____   _____

_____   _____

Is there another name for your topic or a synonym for it? If so, write it here.

Example: rainmaker

_____   _____

Content Connections for Cinquains

Language Arts

Suppose your language arts teacher has asked you to define a vocabulary word you are studying. Your teacher would like you to write your definition as a cinquain. Think about the word you are studying. Think about what the word means. Think about a synonym for the word. Write a cinquain defining a vocabulary word you are studying.

Math

Suppose your math teacher has asked you to describe a geometric shape that you have been studying. Your teacher would like you to write your description as a cinquain. Think about the shape. Think about adjectives to describe its appearance. Think about real objects that are designed in this shape. Think about what the shape can do. Write a cinquain describing the geometric shape.

Content Connections for Cinquains *(cont.)*

Social Studies

Suppose your social studies teacher has asked you to describe the lifestyle of a group of people you are studying. Your teacher would like you to write your description as a cinquain. Think about the group of people you are studying. Think about what the group was called. Think about what the group was like. Think about what the group did. Write a cinquain describing the lifestyle of a group of people you are studying.

Science

Suppose your science teacher has asked you to describe the function of a piece of scientific equipment. Your teacher would like you to write your description as a cinquain. Think about the piece of equipment. Think about how you use it. Think about why you use it. Think about what it is like. Write a cinquain describing the function of a piece of scientific equipment.

Cinquain Response and Assessment Sheet

Author's Name _____

Poem Title _____

Responder's Name(s) _____ Date _____

Responder:

Did the author . . .

❏ use the correct number of words on each line?

❏ use the correct part of speech on each line?

❏ include only words related to the topic?

❏ make sure that the overall poem makes sense?

❏ use the best possible word choice?

Revision suggestions: _____

_____

Author:

Before writing your final copy, have you . . .

❏ made any necessary revisions from your peer response session?

❏ checked for proper spelling?

❏ checked for proper capitalization?

❏ checked for proper punctuation?

Complete the following statements to provide some information about your writing:

I had a hard time _____.

My favorite part of the poem is _____.

I would like to write another cinquain sometime. (Circle one.)

Yes   No

Teacher:

_____ correct format of poem

_____ appropriate word choice

_____ neatness

_____ correct spelling and mechanics

_____ _____

Score: _____

Five Senses Poem

Background for the Teacher

Definition: A five senses poem is a poem in which each line describes a topic as it appeals to one of the senses. Any number of topics could be used with this poem. This lesson will instruct students in writing a five senses poem about their favorite holiday.

Skills Needed: knowledge of the five senses, choosing words which appeal to each of the senses

Materials: reproductions of My Favorite Holiday (page 65) and Holiday Sensations (page 66) worksheets for each student in the class; colored pencils, crayons, or markers; various colors of construction paper; scissors; glue or tape

Preparation: Reproduce the My Favorite Holiday and Holiday Sensations worksheets. Gather other materials needed for the lesson.

Lesson Plan

Prewriting

1. Distribute the My Favorite Holiday worksheet and colored pencils, crayons, or markers. Ask students to each draw a picture of a scene from their favorite holiday. Provide ample time for students to add detail and color to their picture.

2. After pictures are complete, have students share their picture with a partner. They should describe their picture as if they were actually in the scene, telling the partner what they see happening in the picture—what they would smell, what they might taste, what they might feel, what sounds they would hear. As students describe the scene for their partner, they should jot down phrases related to the picture for each of the five senses—sight, sound, taste, smell, and touch.

Drafting

1. Share the sample five senses poem, "Thanksgiving." Point out the structure of the poem in which each line uses a different sense to help create the scene or image. Remind students of the impact of careful, specific word choices.

2. Instruct students to draft their five senses poem, writing a different line for each sense. The final line, relating to the sense of touch, could describe something that can be touched or something that is "felt" emotionally.

Five Senses Poem (cont.)

Revising/Editing

1. When the poem is drafted, students should share their five senses poem with peer responders. Provide the Five Senses Poem Response and Assessment Sheet for this purpose.

   Peer responders should check to ensure that each line describes one of the five senses, that each line begins with a capital letter and ends with a period, and that each line relates to the chosen topic.

2. Following peer response, students should make any necessary revisions before writing a final copy of the poem.

Publishing

1. Have students create a greeting card to celebrate their favorite holiday. Distribute a sheet of construction paper to each student. Have them fold the paper in half. On the outside of the card, students could attach their drawing from the My Favorite Holiday worksheet. On the inside of the card, students could write the final copy of their five senses poem, using the Holiday Sensations worksheet for structure.

2. Completed cards make a clever bulletin board or wall display!

Student Sample of Five Senses Poem

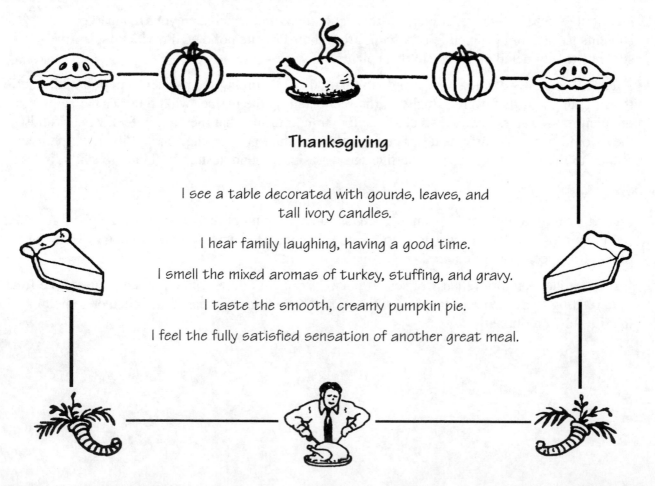

Thanksgiving

I see a table decorated with gourds, leaves, and
tall ivory candles.

I hear family laughing, having a good time.

I smell the mixed aromas of turkey, stuffing, and gravy.

I taste the smooth, creamy pumpkin pie.

I feel the fully satisfied sensation of another great meal.

My Favorite Holiday

Sight:

_____   _____

_____   _____

_____   _____

Sound:

_____   _____

_____   _____

_____   _____

Taste:

_____   _____

_____   _____

_____   _____

Smell:

_____   _____

_____   _____

_____   _____

Feel:

_____   _____

_____   _____

_____   _____

Directions: Complete and illustrate the lines below, using a favorite holiday as inspiration.

Holiday Sensations

I see _____

I hear _____

I taste _____

I smell _____

I feel _____

Content Connections for Five Senses Poems

Language Arts

Suppose your language arts teacher has asked you to pretend you are a character in a story you have been reading. Your teacher would like you to write a five senses poem to describe what you are experiencing in the story. Think about a character from the story. Think about what happens to that character during the story. Think about how you would feel if you were that character. Write a five senses poem as if you were a character in a story you have been reading.

Fine Arts

Suppose your fine arts teacher has asked you to describe how a piece of music or art appeals to each of your five senses. Your teacher would like you to write your impressions as a five senses poem. Think about the piece of music or art you have been studying. Think about each of the five senses in the human body. Think about how the music or art makes you feel. Think about what you see, hear, smell, and taste when you listen to the music or look at the art. Write a five senses poem describing how a piece of music or art that you have been studying appeals to each of your five senses.

Content Connections for
Five Senses Poems *(cont.)*

Social Studies

Suppose your social studies teacher has asked you to pretend that you are experiencing a moment in history that you have been studying. Your teacher would like you to write a five senses poem to describe what you are experiencing. Think about the moment in history that you have been studying. Think about what happened during that time. Think about why certain things took place. Think about how the people during that time felt. Write a five senses poem describing a moment in history that you have been studying.

Science

Suppose your science teacher has asked you to define the functions of each of the five senses of the human body. Your teacher would like you to write your definitions as a five senses poem. Think about each of the five senses of the human body. Think about how we use our senses. Think about why we need each of the senses. Write a five senses poem describing the function of each of the senses of the human body.

Five Senses Poem Response and Assessment Sheet

Author's Name _____

Poem Title _____

Responder's Name(s) _____ Date _____

Responder:

Did the author . . .

❏ use the correct number of words on each line?

❏ use the correct part of speech on each line?

❏ include only words related to the topic?

❏ make sure that the overall poem makes sense?

❏ use the best possible word choice?

Revision suggestions: _____

_____

Author:

Before writing your final copy, have you . . .

❏ made any necessary revisions from your peer response session?

❏ checked for proper spelling?

❏ checked for proper capitalization?

❏ checked for proper punctuation?

Complete the following statements to provide some information about your writing:

I had a hard time _____.

My favorite part of the poem is _____.

I would like to write another cinquain sometime. (Circle one.)

Yes   No

Teacher:

_____ correct format of poem

_____ appropriate word choice

_____ neatness

_____ correct spelling and mechanics

_____ _____

Score: _____

Skill Building: Using Similes

Background for the Teacher

Definition: A simile is a technique for comparing two things using the words *like* or *as*.

Materials: reproductions of Similarities worksheet (page 71)

Preparation: Reproduce the Similarities worksheet for each student in the class.

Lesson Plan

1. Write the words *eyes* and *diamonds* on the chalkboard.

2. Ask students to explain how *eyes* and *diamonds* might be similar. (They will probably say that both can sparkle.)

3. Write the statement "Her eyes were like diamonds" on the board. Explain to students that this is an example of a simile. Define simile as a comparison using the words *like* or *as*.

4. Write two more words on the board, *grass* and *shirt*.

5. Ask students again how the words grass and shirt could be similar. Once students arrive at the correct conclusion, write the following sentence on the chalkboard: "His shirt was as green as grass."

6. Distribute the Similarities worksheet. Review the definition of a simile with the students again. Instruct students to complete the worksheet independently, gaining more practice with writing similes.

Similarities

A simile is a technique for comparing two things. Similes use the words "like" or "as" to show how the items are alike. Here are some similes.

Her teeth are as white as winter snow.
(Her teeth are white, and snow is white.)

The snake was like a garden hose.
(The snake was thin and black and lying in the grass. The garden hose was also thin and black and lying in the grass.)

Directions: Try to explain the comparisons in the following similes:

The baby's cheeks were like a rose.

The baby's cheeks are _____ and a rose is _____.

The full moon is like a cookie.

The full moon is _____ and a cookie is _____.

The baseball whizzed by like a rocket.

The baseball _____ and a rocket _____.

The coffee is like ink.

Coffee is _____ and ink is _____.

Now you try it! Write some similes of your own.

The boat is_____.

The cave is _____.

Her hair is _____.

Read your similes to a friend. See if he or she can explain your comparison.

Color Poem

Background for the Teacher

Definition: A color poem is a poem written using similes to describe a color from every sense—except sight. It requires students to think about a topic that is primarily visual but describe it without using any visual references.

Skills Needed: using similes for comparison, precise word choice

Materials: 3–4 crayons in red, green, blue, yellow, orange, black, purple, white, and brown; reproductions of Sensational Colors worksheet (page 75), Color Poem worksheet (page 76), and Color Poem Response and Assessment Sheet (page 78) for each writing group; scraps of various colored materials, such as cardboard, foil, carpet, burlap; scissors; glue; poster board; markers

Preparation: Reproduce the Sensational Colors worksheet and the Color Poem Response and Assessment Sheet. Gather other materials needed for the lesson.

Lesson Plan

Prewriting

1. Ask students to close their eyes. Call on one student and ask that student to describe what the color red looks like. Most likely, the student will have difficulty and end up saying something like, "Red is red. I don't know!" The student might make comparisons to red objects, saying, "Red is like strawberries or a fire engine." Ask the student to further describe, saying "I don't know what a strawberry looks like. What do you mean?" You may need to assist by offering, "Perhaps red on a strawberry is rough but sweet-tasting."

2. Have students describe another color in the same manner, trying to avoid visual images and instead offering other sensory descriptions—texture, taste, sound, or smell. If a student uses a visual comparison ("Yellow is like the sun."), prompt the student to offer more information using other senses: "Yellow is burning, bright, and hot."

3. Distribute one crayon to each student. Instruct students to sit with other students who have the same color of crayon. This will be their writing group for the color poem.

Drafting

1. Tell students that they will be writing a poem about a color. They are to write the poem as if they were writing it for a person who has a visual handicap. The person may not know what certain objects look like so they cannot write about things that are the color. Instead, instruct students that they are to describe their color from each of the other senses: sound, smell, taste, and feel.

Color Poem *(cont.)*

Drafting *(cont.)*

2. Remind students that they will be using similes to compare their color to different sounds, smells, tastes, and textures.

3. Distribute the Sensational Colors worksheet to each group of students. Review the directions with them before completing the sheet.

4. When groups have completed the brainstorming worksheet, share several sample color poems (page 74) with them. Point out particularly effective word choices. Elicit student feedback regarding the comparisons the authors used. Note the structure of the poems for students.

5. Instruct groups to review their ideas from the Sensational Colors worksheet and select those ideas which make the strongest comparison for each sense. Tell students to use their ideas to draft each line of the color poem. Provide a color poem outline (page 76) for students to use, if necessary, for drafting their poems.

Revising/Editing

1. Once the poems are drafted, students should share their color poems with peer responders. Provide the Color Poem Response and Assessment Sheet for this purpose. Peer responders should check to make sure that each line describes the color through a different sense, that no visual comparisons have been used, and that similes are used in each line. Responders could also make suggestions for stronger word choice as appropriate.

2. Following peer response, students should make any necessary revisions before writing a final copy of the poem.

Publishing

Students could write their final copy of the color poem in the same color ink as their topic and mount it on poster board. They could then cover the poster board with scraps of material that matches their topic color. Try to obtain a wide variety of textured materials such as corduroy, silk, cotton, flannel, wallpaper samples, corrugated paper, carpet samples, etc. This will provide a textured backing to enhance their "non-visual" color poem.

Student Samples of Color Poem

White

White is like the sound of ice cubes clinking in a glass.

White is like the smell of freshly picked daisies from a green, green meadow.

White is like the taste of sweet, creamy ice cream on a hot summer day.

White is like the feel of a soft, fluffy pillow comforting you to sleep.

Blue

Blue smells like the fresh, salty ocean as the breeze blows across it.

Blue sounds like a peaceful river flowing through the forest.

Blue tastes like a slippery, sweet lollipop energizing you in the middle of the afternoon.

Blue feels like soaring through the air with the birds and the clouds.

Brown

Brown is like the taste of rich, thick chocolate as you smooth it around on your tongue.

Brown is like the smell of tangy spices, soaking into barbecued meat.

Brown is like the sound of construction equipment, struggling to move the earth.

Brown is like the feeling of sluggishness, like lying around all day.

Pink

Pink tastes like light, sugary cotton candy you get at the circus.

Pink smells like a baby just after a bath.

Pink sounds like tiny, glass wind chimes blowing in the breeze.

Pink feels like a light feather tickling your skin.

Sensational Colors

Directions: Complete the following items about your color.

First, think of things that are made or come in your chosen color. For example, if you are writing about yellow, a banana, the sun, and a raincoat are all yellow things.

These things are _____:
(your color)

You cannot simply name and write about the things that you just listed in your poem. Just think about the items in your list to help you complete the rest of this worksheet, describing your color by using the other four senses.

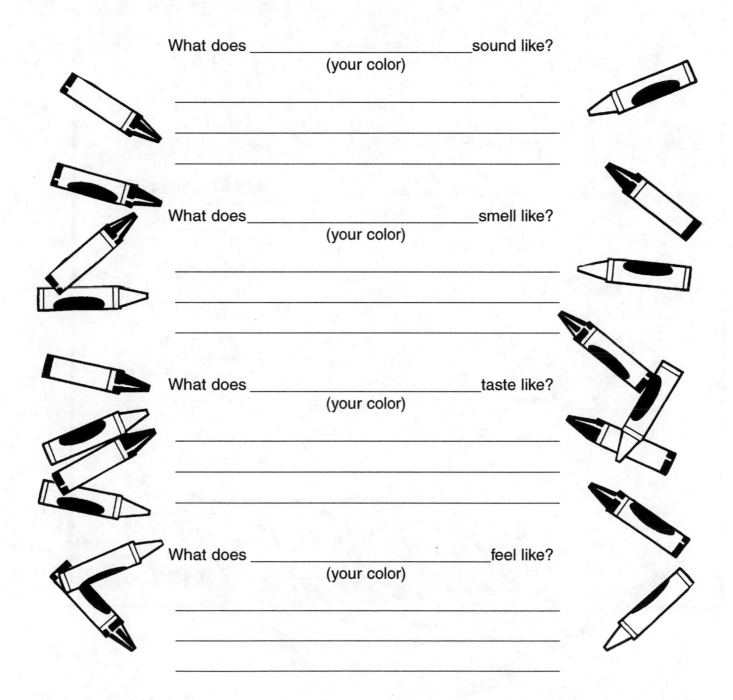

What does _____ sound like?
(your color)

_____

_____

_____

What does _____ smell like?
(your color)

_____

_____

_____

What does _____ taste like?
(your color)

_____

_____

_____

What does _____ feel like?
(your color)

_____

_____

_____

Color Poem

_____

_____is like the sound

of _____.

_____is like the smell

of _____.

_____is like the taste

of _____.

_____is like the feel

of _____.

Content Connections for Color Poems

Suppose your social studies teacher has asked you to describe an abstract concept, such as fear, jealousy, peace, or love. Your teacher would like you to write a poem describing the assigned word in the same manner you described a color. Think about the meaning of the assigned word. Think about how the word makes people feel. Think of objects or people that remind you of the word. Write a poem that describes the assigned word by telling what it smells like, sounds like, tastes like, feels like, and looks like.

(**Example:** Fear is like the smell of . . .)

Suppose your fine arts teacher has asked you to describe a piece of artwork without using any visual references. Your teacher would like you to write a poem describing the art in the same manner you described a color. Think about how the art makes people feel. Think of the smells, sounds, and tastes that the art brings to mind. Write a poem that describes the artwork by what it smells like, sounds like, tastes like, and feels like.

(**Example:** The Mona Lisa is like the sound of . . .)

Color Poem Response and Assessment Sheet

Author's Name _____

Poem Title_____

Responder's Name(s) _____ Date _____

Responder:

Did the author . . .

- ❑ describe the color through a different sense on each line of the poem?
- ❑ use no visual comparisons?
- ❑ use similes to make each comparison? (Look for the words "like" or "as.")
- ❑ use the best possible word choice?

Revision suggestions: _____

_____

Author:

Before writing your final copy, have you . . .

- ❑ made any necessary revisions from your peer response session?
- ❑ checked for proper spelling?
- ❑ checked for proper capitalization?
- ❑ checked for proper punctuation?

Complete the following statements to provide some information about your writing:

I had a hard time _____.

My favorite part of the poem is _____.

I would like to write another color poem sometime. (Circle one.)

                 Yes   No

Teacher:

_____ correct format of poem

_____ appropriate word choice

_____ neatness

_____ correct spelling and mechanics

_____ _____

Score: _____

Skill Building: Using Metaphors

Background for the Teacher

Definitions: A metaphor is a technique for comparing two things. Unlike a simile, a metaphor does not use the words *like* or *as*.

Materials: reproductions of Love-ly Lines worksheet (page 80)

Preparation: Reproduce the Love-ly Lines worksheet for each student.

Lesson Plan

1. Write the words *alarm clock* and *rooster* on the chalkboard or overhead projector.

2. Ask students to explain how an alarm clock and a rooster might be similar. (They will probably say that an alarm clock wakes a person up in the morning like a rooster does when it crows.)

3. Write the statement "My alarm clock is a rooster" on the board. Explain to students that this is an example of a metaphor. Define a metaphor as a comparison that does not use the words *like* or *as*.

4. Expand the comparison by continuing to write "My alarm clock is a rooster, waking me at dawn's first light." Explain that the elaboration helps the comparison make sense to the reader.

5. Distribute the Love-ly Lines worksheet. Review the definition of a metaphor with students again. Instruct students to complete the worksheet independently, gaining more practice with writing metaphors.

Love-ly Lines

Love is a teddy bear. It keeps you warm at night.

Love is a mountain. It makes you feel like you can touch the sky.

Love is a milkshake. Sometimes you need to shake it up a little.

These lines use metaphors to describe love. The writer compares love to something and then explains the connection. The comparison is called a metaphor. The writer is comparing two objects without using the words "like" or "as."

See if you can explain the connection in the following metaphors.

Love is the wind.

_____

Love is a rainbow.

_____

Love is a sail on a sailboat.

_____

Now try to write some metaphors with explanations.

Time is _____

_____.

Friendship is _____

_____.

Anger is _____

_____

Definition Poem

Background for the Teacher

Definition: A definition poem is a free verse which uses metaphors to describe the topic.

Skills Needed: familiarity with metaphors

Materials: reproductions of Definition Poem Web worksheet (page 84) and Definition Response and Assessment Sheet (page 86) for each student or for groups of students (see Prewriting #6, below) several old dictionaries or copies of dictionary pages

Preparation: Reproduce the Definition Poem Web worksheet and the Definition Response and Assessment Sheet. Gather old dictionaries.

Lesson Plan

Prewriting

1. Tell students that a definition poem uses a conceptual topic—something that is not an object, person, or place, but is instead an emotion, feeling, or way of being.

2. On a chart, chalkboard, or overhead projector, help students brainstorm possible conceptual topics. Possible concepts include freedom, jealousy, love, friendship, hope, anger, sadness, independence, time, fear, death, life, etc.

3. Share the student sample, "Hope is . . ." (page 83). Read the poem once for students to gain an idea of the form of the poem, which is free verse.

4. Read the poem a second time, asking students to list each item that the author compares to hope.

5. Review the term *metaphor* with students. Ask students why the author compared hope to each of the items. For example, after reading, "Hope is a tissue, wiping away your problems and fears," ask students, "Why does the author think hope is like a tissue?"

6. Have students select a topic for their poems from the list the class brainstormed during prewriting. (*Note*: Depending on the skill level of your students, you may wish to have students work in groups to write this challenging poem.)

7. Using the Definition Poem Web worksheet, have students make comparisons between their topic and other objects. The web is designed in two tiers: the first offshoot from the topic is for students to write the objects to be compared; the second offshoot is for elaborating on the comparison.

Definition Poem *(cont.)*

Drafting

Once students have generated several comparisons and elaborations, instruct them to begin drafting their definition poem. Review student sample, "Hope is . . ." to show students a possible format for their poem.

Since a definition poem is free verse, students could take liberties with the structure of the poem as long as the metaphors are included and complete.

Revising/Editing

1. When the poem is drafted, students should share their definition poems with peer responders. Provide the Definition Poem Response and Assessment Sheet for this purpose. Peer responders should check to make sure that the topic is compared to several items without using *like* or *as*, that each comparison is elaborated for explanation, and that each comparison makes sense.

2. Following peer response, students should make any necessary revisions before writing a final copy of the poem.

Publishing

Obtain several old dictionaries that can be torn apart or photocopy pages from a dictionary. Have the students use the dictionary pages as backgrounds for their poems since they are writing a type of definition. They should each mount the final copy of their poem on the dictionary page background.

Student Samples of Definition Poems

Sadness is...

Sadness is a black cloud
on the day of your
baseball game.

Sadness is your fish
floating belly up in the
water.

Sadness is losing electricity
when your favorite show is
on TV.

Sadness is a tear
that falls from your face.

Hope is...

Hope is a tissue,
wiping away your problems and fears.

Hope is a bright sun ray,
warming your heart and soul.

Hope is a tattered teddy bear,
hugging your tears, making them
tears of joy.

Hope is a cozy, warm blanket,
protecting you from the problems of
the world.

Hope is a striving flower
in a dried and silty ground.

Hope is a butterfly,
fluttering around a garden of weeds.

Hope is a twinkling star
in a sky of black clouds.

Friends are...

Friends are flowers
brightening your day.

Friends are a gift
picked only for you.

Friends are an energy source
keeping you going all day and night.

Friends are diamonds
you treasure forever.

Definition Poem Web

This web can help you to organize your thoughts and your poem. Here is an example showing how the web was used to help write the poem, "Hope is . . .":

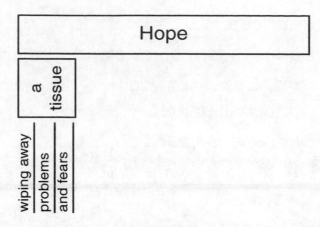

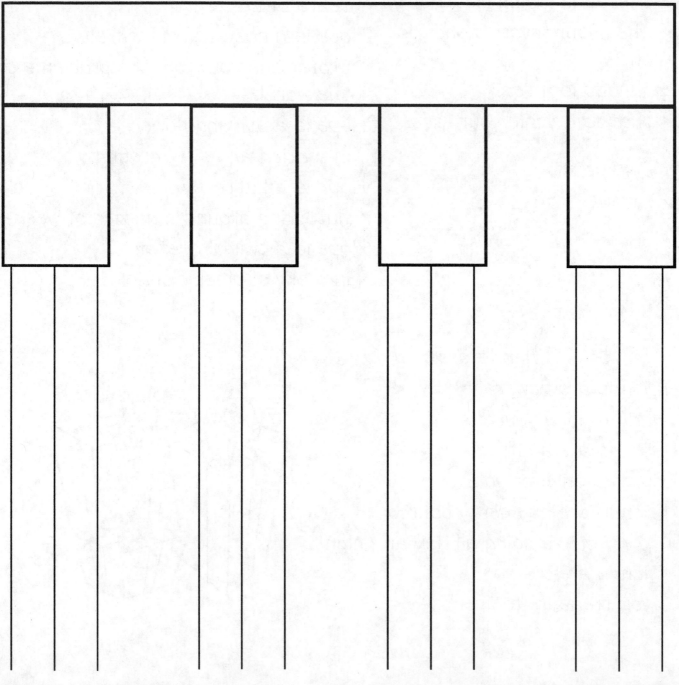

Content Connections for Definition Poems

Math

Suppose your math teacher has asked you to define a math concept such as time or money. Your teacher would like you to write a definition poem defining the math concept. Think about the meaning of the assigned word. Think about comparisons you could make to the concept. Think about what the concept means to people. Write a poem that defines the math concept using comparisons to other objects.

Language Arts

Suppose your language arts teacher has asked you to define an abstract vocabulary word, such as enthusiasm, excitement, or sympathy. Your teacher would like you to write a poem defining the assigned word. Think about the meaning of the assigned word. Think about comparisons you could make to the concept. Think about what the concept means to people. Write a poem that defines the assigned vocabulary word using comparisons to other objects.

Definition Poem Response and Assessment Sheet

Author's Name _____

Poem Title _____

Responder's Name(s) _____ Date _____

Responder:

Did the author . . .

❑ compare several items to the topic?

❑ elaborate to explain each comparison?

❑ choose comparisons that make sense?

❑ use the best possible word choice?

Revision suggestions: _____

_____

Author:

Before writing your final copy, have you . . .

❑ made any necessary revisions from your peer response session?

❑ checked for proper spelling?

❑ checked for proper capitalization?

❑ checked for proper punctuation?

Complete the following statements to provide some information about your writing:

I had a hard time _____.

My favorite part of the poem is _____.

I would like to write another definition poem sometime. (Circle one.)

                    Yes   No

Teacher:

_____ correct format of poem

_____ appropriate word choice

_____ neatness

_____ correct spelling and mechanics

_____ _____

Score: _____

Skill Building: Onomatopoeia

Background for the Teacher

Definition: Onomatopoeia uses words which sound like the objects or actions they are describing.

Materials: reproductions of What's That Sound? worksheet (page 88)

Preparation: Reproduce the What's That Sound? worksheet.

Lesson Plan

1. Define onomatopoeia for students.

2. Distribute the What's That Sound? worksheet. Review the directions on the worksheet and complete the first part of the worksheet with the students. Help students notice that using words for the sounds that animals make are examples of onomatopoeia.

3. Continue the examples of onomatopoeia by completing the second section of the worksheet, writing sounds that specific objects make.

4. To complete the worksheet, assist students in generating sounds that would be heard if they were involved in the actions listed in the third section of the worksheet.

What's That Sound?

What sound does each of the following animals make?

a cat _____

a duck _____

a dog _____

a sheep _____

a horse _____

a snake _____

What sound does each of the following objects make?

a train _____

the ocean _____

a balloon _____

a door _____

the wind _____

thunder _____

Write the sounds you would hear if you were . . .

at a football game _____

trick-or-treating _____

bowling _____

toasting a piece of bread _____

blowing a bubble with bubble gum _____

emptying a dishwasher _____

listening to a thunderstorm _____

watching fireworks _____

waking up _____

running to answer a ringing phone _____

hitting a home run _____

Event Poem

Background for the Teacher

Definition: An event poem captures the actions and sounds of a specific event or action.

Skills Needed: understanding of onomatopoeia, sequencing events

Materials: reproductions of Sequence of Events worksheet (page 92) and Event Poem Response and Assessment Sheet (page 94), overhead transparency of Sequence of Events worksheet, chart paper or chalkboard, cassette tape and tape recorders

Preparation: Reproduce the Sequence of Events worksheet and the Event Poem Response and Assessment Sheet. Prepare overhead transparency of the Sequence of Events worksheet. Gather other materials needed for the lesson.

Lesson Plan

Prewriting

1. Review the list of events presented in the onomatopoeia lesson What's That Sound? worksheet (page 88):

    - at a football game
    - trick-or-treating
    - bowling
    - toasting a piece of bread
    - blowing a bubble with bubble gum
    - hitting a home run

    - listening to a thunderstorm
    - watching fireworks
    - waking up
    - running to answer a ringing phone
    - emptying a dishwasher

2. Have students select one event with which they are familiar to use as the topic of their event poem.

Drafting

1. Using an overhead transparency of the Sequence of Events graphic organizer, sequence the steps of a specific event such as making brownies from a boxed mix:

    Get the brownies box out of the pantry.

    Turn the oven on.

    Open the box.

    Dump the mix in the bowl.

    Add eggs, water, and oil.

    Stir.

    Grease a baking pan.

    Pour the mixture in the pan.

    Place pan in the oven and set the timer.

    Wait.

    The timer goes off.

    Remove the brownies from the oven and let them cool.

    Eat!

Event Poem *(cont.)*

Drafting *(cont.)*

Write each of these steps in a box on the transparency of the Sequence of Events worksheet to model the procedure that students will use in sequencing their chosen event.

2. Distribute the Sequence of Events worksheet to each student. Instruct students to follow the same process to sequence the actions or steps of the event they have chosen.

3. Once students have sequenced the steps of their topic, return to your model of brownie making. On chart paper or the chalkboard, rewrite the sequence of steps in brownie making, skipping a line between each step. Instruct students to do the same to their topic as you complete the brownie example.

4. Once the steps have been rewritten in draft form, show students how to add onomatopoeia to their event poem. On the skipped lines, add one or two onomatopoeic words to describe the actions of the previous line. For example:

Get the brownie box out of the pantry.

creak, hmmmm

Turn on the oven.

click, poof

Open the box.

rip, zip

Dump the mix in a bowl.

plop, poof

and so forth.

5. Instruct students to complete the draft of their event poem by adding onomatopoeic words on the skipped lines of their sequenced steps.

Revising/Editing

1. When the poem is drafted, students should share their event poems with peer responders. Provide the Event Poem Response and Assessment Sheet for this purpose. Peer responders should check to make sure the steps are properly sequenced, that appropriate onomatopoeia is added between every line, and that the poem captures the overall actions and sounds of the event.

2. Following peer response, students should make any necessary revisions before writing a final copy of the poem.

Publishing

1. Have students tape-record their final poem, using their voices or any props to add the necessary onomatopoeia sound effects. You may wish to assign this as homework so that students have access to a wider variety of sound-making devices.

2. You could keep all of the tapes in a listening center in your classroom for students to hear the work of their classmates.

Student Samples of Event Poems

The Fight

"Get off me!"
        slap, kick
"Don't shove me!"
        Bop! Zap!
"Stop it, turnip brain!"
        moan, groan
"That's what you get!"
        giggle, snicker
"Ooh, my nose!"
        scream, sob
"There's blood!"
        squeeze, hold
"I'm telling Mom!"
        stomp, run.

The Home Run

Walk up to the plate,
Breathe in, breathe out
Concentrate
First pitch
            ZOOM!
Caught looking.
Darn!
Breathe in, breathe out
Concentrate
Second pitch
    Flop—hit the dirt.
Third pitch
WHOOSH!
YEAH!
ROAR!
It's outta here!

Wake Up

"ZZZZZZzzzzzz"
    lie, snore
"RRRRRRrrrrring!"
    roll, sigh
"RRRRRRrrrrring!"
    slap, smack
"ZZZZZZzzzzzz"
    breathe, breathe
"RRRRRrrrrrring!"
    swat, throw
"RRRRRRRrrrring!"
        Oh, no
Too far away.
Have to get up.

Sequence of Events

Write your event topic here. _____

Imagine you are participating in your chosen event. Think of what would happen first, second, third, etc. Write each step of the event in one of the boxes. Follow the sequence chain to keep the pieces of action in order.

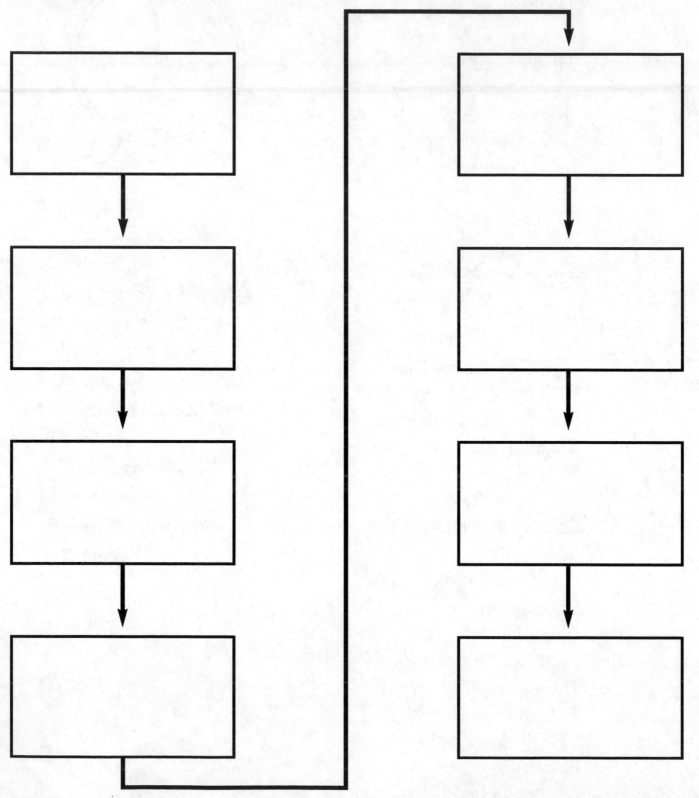

Content Connections for Event Poems

Math

Suppose your math teacher has asked you to sequence the steps in solving a particular math problem. Your teacher would like you to write an event poem to sequence the steps. Think about what you do first to solve the problem. Think about each step that follows. Think about the final step toward solving the problem. Write an event poem that sequences the steps for solving a particular math problem.

Science

Suppose your science teacher has asked you to sequence the steps in conducting a particular scientific experiment. Your teacher would like you to write an event poem to sequence the steps. Think about what you do first to conduct the experiment. Think about each step that follows. Think about the final step for conducting the experiment. Write an event poem that sequences the steps for conducting a particular scientific experiment.

Event Poem Response and Assessment Sheet

Author's Name _____

Poem Title _____

Responder's Name(s) _____ Date _____

Responder:

Did the author . . .

❑ sequence the events properly?

❑ use onomatopoeia between every line of action?

❑ capture the overall actions and sounds of the event?

❑ use the best possible word choice?

Revision suggestions: _____

_____

Author:

Before writing your final copy, have you . . .

❑ made any necessary revisions from your peer response session?

❑ checked for proper spelling?

❑ checked for proper capitalization?

❑ checked for proper punctuation?

Complete the following statements to provide some information about your writing:

I had a hard time _____.

My favorite part of the poem is _____.

I would like to write another event poem sometime. (Circle one.)

Yes   No

Teacher:

_____ correct format of poem

_____ appropriate word choice

_____ neatness

_____ correct spelling and mechanics

_____ _____

Score: _____

Skill Building: Using Line Breaks and White Space

Background for the Teacher

Definition: Students will learn to arrange words in a poem, deliberately attending to white space on the paper and appropriate places to break lines. This lesson is particularly helpful for those students who just can't seem to write poetry that doesn't rhyme. This skill helps them understand how to break lines so that ideas written in prose turn into a poem quite easily.

Materials: none

Preparation: no special preparation needed

Lesson Plan

1. Use a whole-class round-robin technique to generate a list of nouns by going around the room and having students state a noun to be added to the class list you are creating. Encourage students to think of specific and unusual nouns.

2. Once you have a sufficient list, ask students to choose one of the nouns to use as a subject in a sentence.

3. Instruct students to write a sentence that contains exactly eight words—no more, no less!

4. Place the following designs on the chalkboard:

Skill Building: Using Line Breaks and White Space *(cont.)*

Lesson Plan *(cont.)*

5. Have students rewrite their sentences several different ways. Instruct them to use each of the patterns from the previous page, placing one word on each line, using the same order of words they created for their sentence. When students are finished, they will have rewritten their sentence in three different poem patterns. Allow students to create other patterns in which to write their sentence if time allows.

6. Ask students to read each of the pattern poems aloud to a partner, pausing at the end of each line. Have them notice if the different patterns make the sentence sound different. (Most likely, students will pause at appropriate times as they read the sentence in the different poem forms, but you may need to model this step.)

7. Explain to students that creating a poem is simple—authors can take sentences or paragraphs and, by breaking them into phrases and lines at natural pauses, create a poem.

8. Repeat the same process by generating a class list of adjectives.

9. Have students select three of the adjectives and create a 15-word sentence using their selected adjectives.

10. Instruct students to rewrite their 15-word sentences in the following patterns:

_____

_____   _____

_____   _____   _____

_____   _____   _____   _____

_____   _____   _____   _____   _____

_____

_____   _____   _____   _____

_____   _____   _____   _____

_____   _____   _____

_____   _____

_____

Skill-Building: Using Line Breaks and White Space *(cont.)*

Lesson Plan *(cont.)*

11. Again, ask students to note which pattern created the best poem for their sentence.

12. Introduce the concept of white space by reading the following sentences and then showing the same sentences as they were turned into poems.

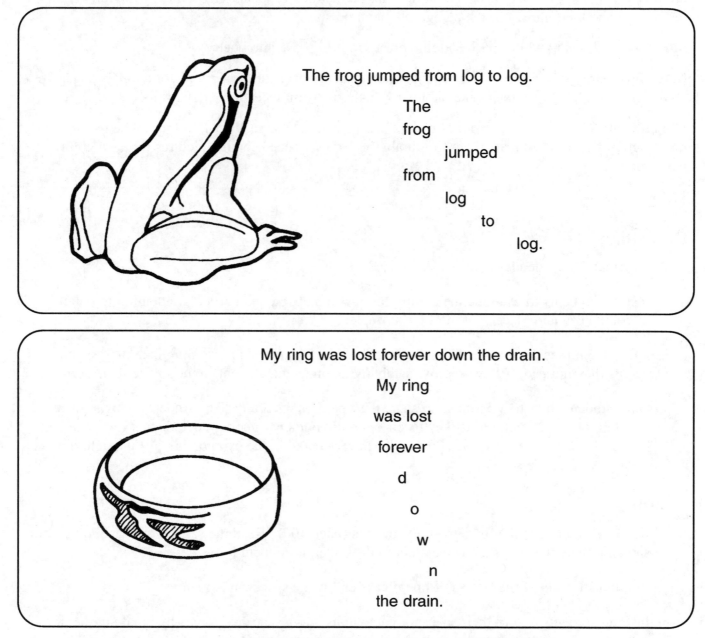

The frog jumped from log to log.

> The
> frog
>   jumped
> from
>   log
>   to
>   log.

My ring was lost forever down the drain.

> My ring
>
> was lost
>
> forever
>
> d
>
> o
>
> w
>
> n
>
> the drain.

13. Ask students if they notice anything unusual about the way the author wrote the words in these poems. Elicit ideas to explain why the author chose to create the lines that way.

14. Explain that authors sometimes use creativity in their poems' layouts by using spacing and white space to create an effect.

Snapshot Poem

Background for the Teacher

Definition: A snapshot poem is one that describes a picture. Students first write a paragraph describing the picture and then transform the paragraph into a poem.

Skills Needed: using white space and line breaks to turn prose into poetry

Materials: various pictures from calendars (nature scenes or pictures of people or animals engaged in an activity work best; use magazine photos as an alternative if calendars are unavailable.)

Preparation: Gather pictures from calendars or magazines. You may wish to mount the pictures on construction paper or laminate them for durability. You will need enough pictures for each child to have one.

Lesson Plan

Prewriting

1. Distribute one calendar picture to each student.

2. Instruct students to examine the picture for one minute, paying particular attention to details such as color, size, and placement of objects/people.

3. After one minute, instruct students to describe their picture in a paragraph, including specific details they noticed. Allow approximately five minutes for students to complete their exercise.

4. Have students turn to a partner and share their paragraphs orally. The students who are listening should look at the pictures as they listen and point out any important details that the writers may have missed. (It is not necessary to include every detail in the paragraph—just enough to paint a clear picture of the scene.)

Drafting

1. Read a sample snapshot paragraph to students (page 100). Read the same words again, this time showing them the snapshot as the author has written it in poem form.

2. Remind students of the effects of line breaks and white spaces in a poem.

3. Instruct students to turn their snapshot paragraphs into a snapshot poems by breaking the lines at natural spots and deliberately arranging the words on the page.

Snapshot Poem *(cont.)*

Revising/Editing

1. When the poem is drafted, students should share their snapshot poem with peer responders. Provide the Snapshot Poem Response and Assessment Sheet for this purpose.

2. Peer responders should check to ensure that the author has divided lines in a logical, natural manner; that words are arranged on the paper appropriately; and that the best possible descriptive words have been used.

3. Following peer response, students should make any necessary revisions before writing a final copy of the poem.

Publishing

Collect the students' final copies of their snapshot poems and create a class book in a calendar format using their picture prompts and the poems that they created. You could bind the pictures and poems together and hang the calendar compilation in the classroom. Since the calendar will be without traditional day or month markings, students could flip the calendar anytime to read a new poem as often as desired.

Student Samples of Snapshot Poems

Original paragraph

The gently sloping grass frames the mountainside majestically. The sun burns down on the mountaintop snow, making it shine like a pile of diamonds. Down below is a valley littered with colorful flowers and small trees. To the right is a brightly lit town, alive with people and music. To the left is a secluded forest lying silent as a tomb.

Contrast

The gently sloping grass
frames the mountainside
          majestically.

The sun burns down
on the mountaintop snow
making it shine like a pile of
                    diamonds.

Down below is a valley
littered with colorful flowers
and
small
trees.

To the right
is a brightly lit town
     alive with people and music.

To the left
is a secluded forest
lying silent as a
tomb.

Original paragraph

As I stand at the frozen windowsill, sipping a steaming cup of chocolate, I gaze out over a snow-covered bridge. The tiny stream that usually trickles down over the jagged rocks is now frozen stiff underneath the falling snow. An old, forest-green wagon sits lonely in the middle of the yard, blanketed with snowflakes. The enormous evergreens playfully lean to one side from the weight of the snowfall the night before. The countryside sparkles, no matter what season it is.

Reminder

As I stand at the frozen
    windowsill, sipping a steaming
    cup of chocolate,
I gaze out over a snow-covered
    bridge.
The tiny stream that usually
    trickles down over the jagged
    rocks is now frozen stiff
    underneath the falling snow.
An old, forest-green wagon sits

lonely in the middle of the yard,
    blanketed with snowflakes.
The enormous evergreens playfully
    lean to one side from the
    weight of the snowfall the night
    before.
The countryside sparkles, no
    matter what season it is.

Content Connections for Snapshot Poems

Suppose your social studies teacher has asked you to describe the scene of a historical event you are studying. Your teacher would like you to write a snapshot poem describing the scene of the event. Think about where and when the historical event took place. Think about specific buildings or people that may have been in the scene. Think about the land surrounding the scene. Write a snapshot poem that describes the scene of a historical event you are studying.

Suppose your social studies teacher has asked you to describe a location in your state or community. Your teacher would like you to write a snapshot poem describing the location. Think about specific buildings or people that may be in that location. Think about the land surrounding the location. Write a snapshot poem that describes a specific location in your state or community.

Content Connections for Snapshot Poems *(cont.)*

Science

Suppose your science teacher has asked you to describe a particular photograph in a textbook you are reading. Your teacher would like you to write a snapshot poem describing the photograph. Think about the location of the photograph. Think about particular people, places, or things that are captured in the photograph. Write a snapshot poem that describes the photograph in your textbook.

Fine Arts

Suppose your fine arts teacher has asked you to describe a particular piece of art you are studying. Your teacher would like you to write a snapshot poem describing the artwork. Think about the colors used in the artwork. Think about the shape of the art. Think about particular people, places, or things that are captured in the artwork. Write a snapshot poem that describes the particular piece of art you are studying.

Snapshot Poem Response and Assessment Sheet

Author's Name _____

Poem Title_____

Responder's Name(s) _____ Date _____

Responder:

Did the author . . .

❏ break the lines at logical and natural places?

❏ arrange the words on the paper appropriately?

❏ uses the best possible word choice?

Revision suggestions: _____

_____

Author:

Before writing your final copy, have you . . .

❏ made any necessary revisions from your peer-response session?

❏ checked for proper spelling?

❏ checked for proper capitalization?

❏ checked for proper punctuation?

Complete the following statements to provide some information about your writing:

I had a hard time _____.

My favorite part of the poem is _____.

I would like to write another snapshot poem sometime. (Circle one.)

                     Yes   No

Teacher:

_____ correct format of poem

_____ appropriate word choice

_____ neatness

_____ correct spelling and mechanics

_____ _____

Score: _____

Concrete Poem

Background for the Teacher

Definition: A concrete poem is a single line of poetry written in the shape of the object being described.

Skills Needed: no special skills needed

Materials: overhead transparency of student samples, stencils of common objects or shapes, colored pencils

Preparation: Create an overhead transparency of student samples. Gather other materials needed for the lesson.

Lesson Plan

Prewriting

1. Show students several student samples of concrete poems.

2. Ask students what makes the concrete poem interesting. If students have difficulty realizing that the poem is written in the shape of the poem topic, trace the outline of the object for the students. Help students notice, too, that the concrete poems only contain one line of poetry.

3. Allow students some time to brainstorm an appropriate topic for their concrete poem. Try to discourage them from selecting something with a detailed or complicated shape. (If you have stencils available, you may wish to encourage students to select a topic for which you have a stencil of its shape.)

Drafting

Since the text of the concrete poem is basically free verse, allow students adequate time to generate their line of poetry. You may wish to encourage students to use alliteration or onomatopoeia to make their poem even more interesting.

Revising/Editing

1. When the poem is drafted, students should share their concrete poem with a peer responder. Provide the Concrete Poem Response and Assessment Sheet for this purpose. Peer responders should check to make sure that only one line of text is used and that the poem is written in the shape of the topic of the poem.

2. Following peer response, students should make any necessary revisions before writing a final copy of the poem.

Publishing

The concrete poem is naturally in publishable form once students write their line in the shape of the topic. Students could use colored pencils to sketch a light background, if desired, to add to the effect of the concrete poem.

Student Samples of Concrete Poems

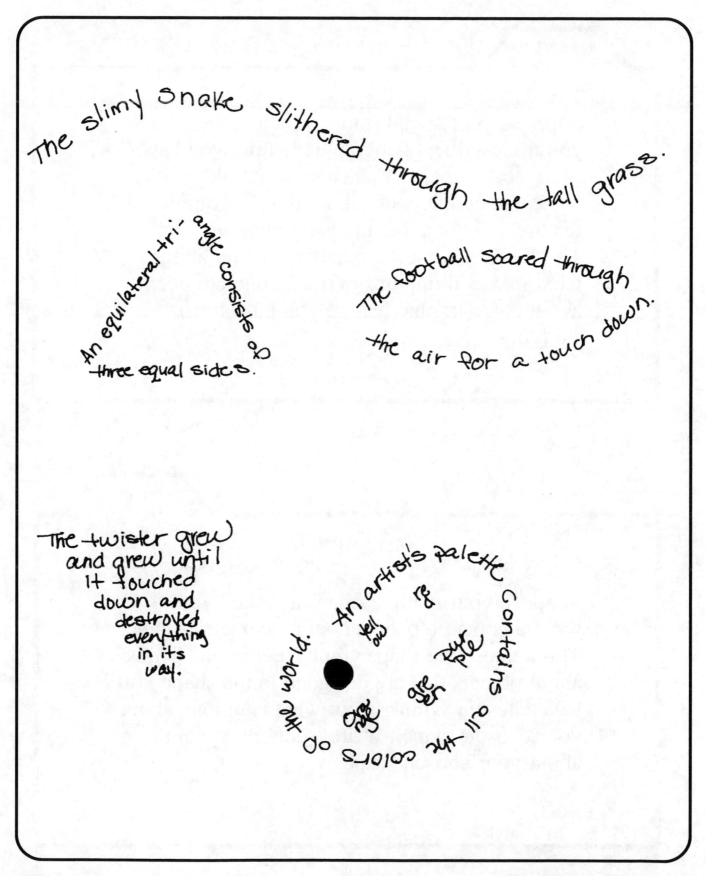

The slimy snake slithered through the tall grass.

An equilateral triangle consists of three equal sides.

The football soared through the air for a touchdown.

The twister grew and grew until it touched down and destroyed everything in its way.

An artist's palette contains all the colors of the world.

Content Connections for Concrete Poems

Social Studies

Suppose your social studies teacher has asked you to describe a geographic feature you have been studying. Your teacher would like you to write a concrete poem about the geographic feature. Think about the geographic feature. Think about what it looks like. Think about what makes it unique. Write a concrete poem about a geographic feature you have been studying.

Math

Suppose your math teacher has asked you to write a concrete poem about a geometric shape. Think about the shape you have chosen. Think about objects that are designed in the shape you have chosen. Think about what is unique about your chosen shape. Write a concrete poem about your chosen shape.

Concrete Poem Response and Assessment Sheet

Author's Name _____

Poem Title _____

Responder's Name(s) _____ Date _____

Responder:

Did the author . . .

- ❏ use only one line of text?
- ❏ write the poem in the shape of the topic?
- ❏ include only words related to the topic?
- ❏ use the best possible word choice?

Revision suggestions: _____

_____

Author:

Before writing your final copy, have you . . .

- ❏ made any necessary revisions from your peer response session?
- ❏ checked for proper spelling?
- ❏ checked for proper capitalization?
- ❏ checked for proper punctuation?

Complete the following statements to provide some information about your writing:

I had a hard time _____.

My favorite part of the poem is _____.

I would like to write another concrete poem sometime. (Circle one.)

    Yes   No

Teacher:

_____ correct format of poem

_____ appropriate word choice

_____ neatness

_____ correct spelling and mechanics

_____ _____

Score: _____

State Poem

Background for the Teacher

Definition: A state poem uses repetition of key words or phrases to create a type of list poem that describes the state itself. The repeated text is cut in the shape of the state for the final copy.

Skills Needed: no special skills needed

Materials: reproductions of State Statements worksheet (page 110) and State Poem Response and Assessment Sheet (page 114), stencils of the shape of your state for students to trace

Preparation: Reproduce the State Statements worksheet and the State Poem Response and Assessment Sheet for each student in the class. Obtain or make an outline or stencil of the shape of your state. (You may need to enlarge a map or other small outline of your state, using an overhead or opaque projector.) Create several copies of the state outline on heavy tagboard or cardboard.

Lesson Plan

Prewriting/Drafting

1. Call on several students to answer the following questions:

   - What is your favorite place to visit in our state?
   - What famous person is from our state?
   - What is the largest city in our state?
   - What is our state known for?
   - Where is your favorite place to vacation in our state?
   - What is a large tourist attraction in our state?

2. Tell students that they will be using their state as the topic of their poem.

3. Distribute the State Statements worksheet. Review the directions with students and allow them to complete it independently or with a partner.

4. When students have completed the worksheet, call on several students to share some of their answers. Instruct the class to add new information to their worksheets if a student mentions a fact they haven't written.

State Poem *(cont.)*

Revising/Editing

1. When the students have completed all of the State Statements, have students share their words and phrases with a peer responder. Provide the State Poem Response and Assessment Sheet for this purpose. Peer responders should check to make sure that each word or phrase from the State Statements worksheet relates to the state and that all words are spelled correctly.

2. Following peer response, students should make any necessary revisions before writing a final copy of the poem.

Publishing

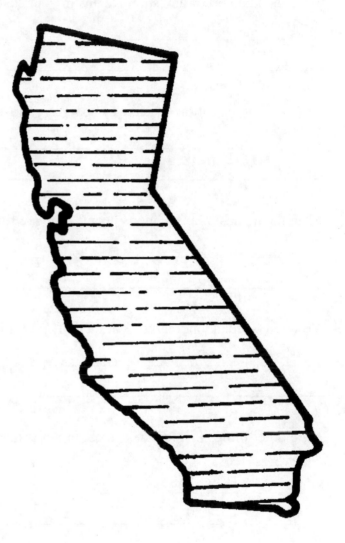

1. Show students a sample of a state poem written in the shape of a state (page 111).

2. Instruct students to follow the directions in the final paragraph of the State Statements worksheet by writing their answers to the questions over and over again (see page 111). The students should write their answers enough times to fill up an entire sheet of paper. (Students can also use a word processing program to type their answers one time and then copy and paste the answers over and over again to fill the page.)

3. When the paper is entirely filled with their state words, have students place a stencil of the shape of their state over their paper. Instruct students to trace and cut out the shape of their state. Reassure students that although some words will be cut off by the stencil, the same word will occur several times in the part of the poem that fits into the shape of the state.

State Statements

Write the name of your state here. _____

Write the capital of your state here. _____

Write the names of three other cities/towns in your state.

_____   _____   _____

Write the name(s) of any sports teams in your state here.

_____   _____

_____   _____

Write favorite vacation or getaway spots in your state here.

_____   _____

_____   _____

Write the names of any famous people who are from your state here.

_____   _____

_____   _____

Write any special landmarks or attractions that are in your state here.

_____   _____

_____   _____

Write other things that are special about your state here. (Do not write in sentences; use single words or phrases.)

_____

_____

_____

_____

_____

Now, write all of these words or phrases over and over again, in a pattern, on a sheet of paper. When you fill the entire page, place a stencil of your state's shape over your paper and trace the shape. Cut out the shape, and you will have a poem about your state in the shape of your state!

State Poem

If you cut along the outline, you will create a state poem about Maryland.

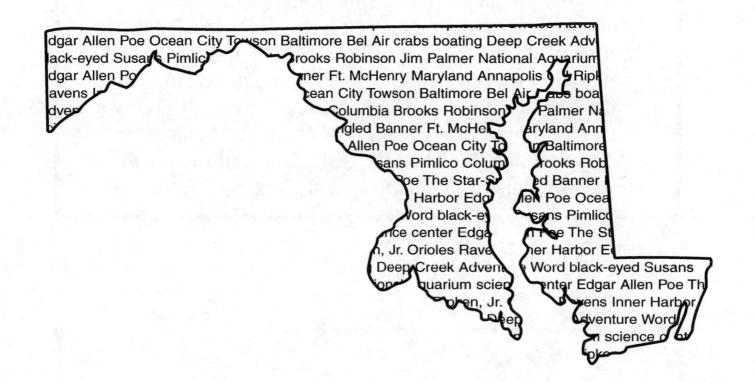

Content Connections for Poems Similar to State Poems

Language Arts

Suppose your language arts teacher has asked you to describe a character from a story you have been reading. Your teacher would like you to write a poem about the character that is similar to a state poem. Think about the character you have selected. Think about what your character looks like. Think about how your character acts. Think about what your character likes to do. Think about what makes your character unique. Write a poem about your character. When you have finished the text portion of the poem, trace the shape of a person over the text and cut it out!

Math

Suppose your math teacher has asked you to write a poem about a geometric shape. Your teacher would like you to write a poem about a shape that is written similarly to a state poem. Think about the shape you have chosen. Think about objects that are designed in the shape you have chosen. When you have finished listing objects that are the shape you have selected, trace the shape over the text and cut it out!

Content Connections for
Poems Similar to State Poems *(cont.)*

Social Studies

Suppose your social studies teacher has asked you to list specific names of a geographic feature you are studying (for example, names of rivers, such as the Amazon, Nile, Mississippi, etc.) Your teacher would like you to write a poem about the geographic feature that is written similar to a state poem. Think about the geographic feature you have selected. Think about specific names of your feature; you may need to consult a map or atlas for ideas. Write a poem about your geographic feature. When you have finished the text portion of the poem, trace the shape of the feature over the text and cut it out!

Science

Suppose your science teacher has asked you to write a poem about things in the ocean. Your teacher would like you to write about the ocean in a poem that is written similar to a state poem. Think about things that can be found in the ocean. When you have finished listing items that can be found in the ocean, trace the shape of an ocean wave over the text and cut it out!

State Poem Response and Assessment Sheet

Author's Name _____

Poem Title _____

Responder's Name(s) _____ Date _____

Responder:

Did the author . . .

❑ use words that relate to his or her state?

❑ spell each word correctly?

❑ capitalize proper nouns (names of people and places)?

Revision suggestions: _____

_____

Author:

Before writing your final copy, have you . . .

❑ made any necessary revisions from your peer response session?

❑ checked for proper spelling?

❑ checked for proper capitalization?

Complete the following statements to provide some information about your writing:

I had a hard time _____.

My favorite part of the poem is _____.

I would like to write another state poem sometime. (Circle one.)

Yes   No

Teacher:

_____ correct format of poem

_____ appropriate word choice

_____ neatness

_____ correct spelling and mechanics

_____ _____

Score: _____

Alphabet Poem

Background for the Teacher

Definition: An alphabet poem is one that is written about a single topic and incorporates words beginning with each letter of the alphabet. The words are written in alphabetical order in a list format. For a challenge, rather than including alphabetical words in a list, words could be written in phrases, that incorporate a word beginning with each letter of the alphabet in order.

Skills Needed: alphabetical order

Materials: reproductions of Alphabet Squares (page 118), Alphabet Poem Brainstorming worksheet (page 119), Alphabet Poem Draft worksheet (page 120), Alphabet Poem Response and Assessment Sheet (page 123), old magazines and newspapers

Preparation: Cut out the alphabet squares from the reproducible. Reproduce the Alphabet Poem Brainstorming worksheet, the Alphabet Poem Draft worksheet, and the Alphabet Poem Response and Assessment Sheet for each student in the class. Gather other materials needed for the lesson.

Lesson Plan

Prewriting

1. Assign each child a different letter of the alphabet by distributing the alphabet squares. If you have more than 26 students, some could work in pairs. If you have fewer than 26 students, some may need to be assigned more than one letter.

2. Select a topic from the Poet Tree bulletin board (see page 9) or have the class generate a single topic. Write the topic on the chalkboard for all students to see.

3. Instruct each student to write one word that comes to mind that is related to the given topic and that begins with the letter on the square of paper. Students could use the back of the square to jot down the word.

Drafting

1. Call each letter of the alphabet, one at a time, in alphabetical order. As a letter is called, the student with that letter should write the word on the chalkboard.

2. When all letters have been called and words are written in order on the chalkboard, read the poem aloud and explain to the class that they have just created an alphabet poem.

3. Ask students to tell you how the poem was generated. (They should say something like, "We picked a topic and then wrote one word about that topic for each letter of the alphabet. Then we put the words in alphabetical order to form the poem.")

Alphabet Poem *(cont.)*

Drafting *(cont.)*

4. Distribute Alphabet Poem Brainstorming worksheets to students. Instruct them to follow the same process the class just used to generate an alphabet poem. Students should select a topic and generate at least one word related to the topic for each letter of the alphabet. Some tricky letters such as *X* could require some creative thinking. Students could use words that begin with the /x/ sound (e.g., *X-traordinary, X-cellent, X-citing*, etc.). Students may also consult the dictionary for ideas.

5. When students have completed the brainstorming sheet, distribute the Alphabet Poem Draft worksheet. Instruct students to write their alphabet poem on this sheet. If they have generated more than one word for each letter of the alphabet, now is the time to choose the best word for the poem. Remind students that only one word per letter should be used.

Revising/Editing

1. When the poem is drafted, students should share their alphabet poems with peer responders. Provide the Alphabet Poem Response and Assessment Sheet for this purpose. Peer responders should check to make sure one word is used for each letter of the alphabet, the words are written in alphabetical order, each line begins with a new word and a capital letter, and each word relates to the chosen topic. Responders could provide suggestions for stronger words to replace other words with the same letter in the draft poem.

2. Following peer response, students should make any necessary revisions before writing a final copy of the poem.

Publishing

Students could write their final copy of the Alphabet Poem and illustrate it with letters cut out from magazines or newspapers.

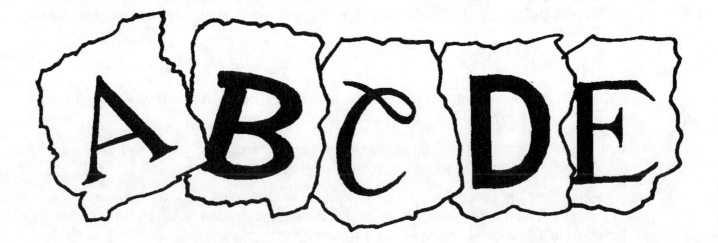

Student Samples of Alphabet Poems

Sports

Awesome
Bats
Catcher
Dribble
Entertainment
Fans
Golf
Home run
Intermission
Jockey
Kick
Linebacker
Money
Net
Overtime
Pitcher
Quick
Runner
Safe
Touchdown
Umpire
Victory
Winner
X-tra innings
Yelling
Zipping bases

Foods

Apple
Banana
Celery
Donuts
Eggplant
French fries
Grapes
Hot dog
Ice cream
Jelly beans
Ketchup
Lemon
Meat
Nuts
Orange
Pasta
Quick oatmeal
Rice
Sausage
Toast
Undercooked carrots
Vegetable
Watermelon
X-tra helpings
Yolk
Zip your lips—no more food!

Alphabet Squares

Reproduce this sheet and cut the squares apart to distribute to students.

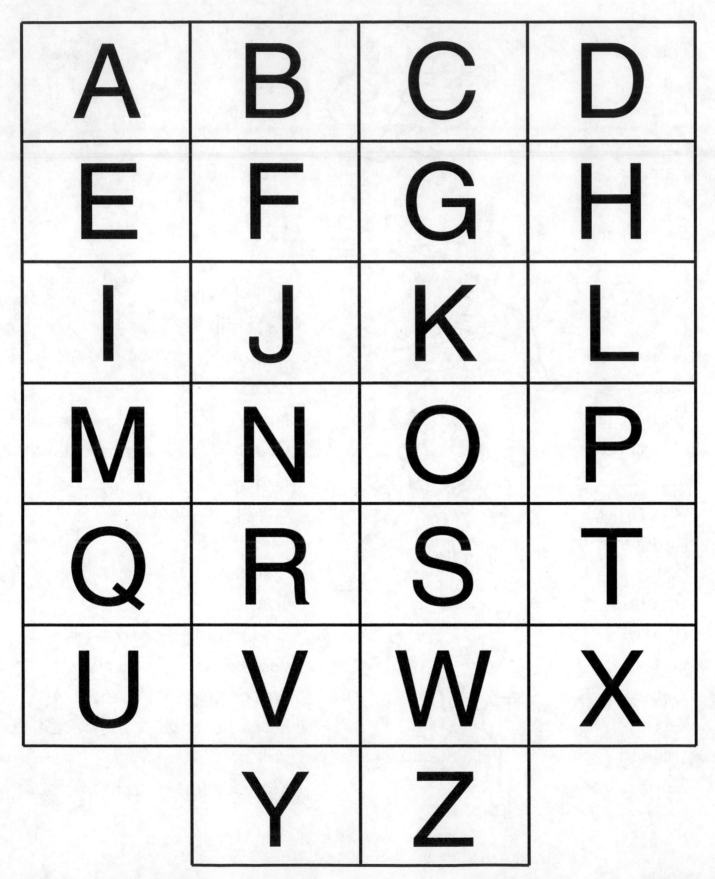

Alphabet Poem Brainstorming

Select a topic: _____

This will become the title of your alphabet poem.

Now, brainstorm words that relate to your topic. You will need words that begin with each letter of the alphabet. If you get stuck with difficult letters like X, you can use words that start with the /x/ sound (for example, X-traordinary).

A _____   J _____   S _____

_____   _____   _____

B _____   K _____   T _____

_____   _____   _____

C _____   L _____   U _____

_____   _____   _____

D _____   M _____   V _____

_____   _____   _____

E _____   N _____   W _____

_____   _____   _____

F _____   O _____   X _____

_____   _____   _____

G _____   P _____   Y _____

_____   _____   _____

H _____   Q _____   Z _____

_____   _____   _____

I _____   R _____

_____   _____

Alphabet Poem Draft

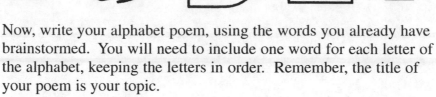

Now, write your alphabet poem, using the words you already have brainstormed. You will need to include one word for each letter of the alphabet, keeping the letters in order. Remember, the title of your poem is your topic.

_____

_____   _____

_____   _____

_____   _____

_____   _____

_____   _____

_____   _____

_____   _____

Content Connections for Alphabet Poems

Suppose your language arts teacher has asked you to brainstorm many examples of a particular part of speech (nouns, verbs, adjectives, etc). Your teacher would like you to write an alphabet poem about the assigned part of speech. Think of the definition of your part of speech. Think of words that start with each letter of the alphabet and are examples of your assigned part of speech. When you have a word for every letter, list your examples in poem form. You have created an alphabet poem!

Suppose your language arts teacher has asked you to brainstorm ideas for character names for your writing assignments. Your teacher would like you to write an alphabet poem using interesting names for characters. Think of a character name that starts with each letter of the alphabet (you may need to take a survey or consult a baby names book or telephone book). When you have a character name for every letter, list your examples in poem form. You have created an alphabet poem!

Content Connections for
Alphabet Poems *(cont.)*

Social Studies

Suppose your social studies teacher has asked you to brainstorm as many words as you can think of related to a topic you are going to be studying. Your teacher would like you to write an alphabet poem about the topic you are going to be studying (your teacher wants to see what you already know about the topic). Think of as many words as you can about the topic you are going to be studying. Since it is a new unit, you may not be able to think of something for every letter. Do the best you can! When you have exhausted your brain, list your words in poem form. You have created an alphabet poem!

Fine Arts

Suppose your drama teacher has asked you to brainstorm ideas for ways people can move. Your teacher would like you to write an alphabet poem using as many ways of moving as you can imagine (skip, gallop, tumble, etc.). Think of as many ways of moving as you can. When you have a word for every letter of the alphabet, list your examples in poem form. You have created an alphabet poem!

Alphabet Poem Response and Assessment Sheet

Author's Name _____

Poem Title _____

Responder's Name(s) _____ Date _____

Responder:

Did the author . . .

- ❑ include one word for each letter of the alphabet?
- ❑ write the words in alphabetical order?
- ❑ place one word on each line?
- ❑ begin each line with a capital letter?
- ❑ include only words related to the topic?
- ❑ use the best possible word choice?

Revision suggestions: _____

_____

Author:

Before writing your final copy, have you . . .

- ❑ made any necessary revisions from your peer response session?
- ❑ checked for proper spelling?
- ❑ checked for capitalization?
- ❑ checked for proper punctuation?

Complete the following statements to provide some information about your writing:

I had a hard time _____.

My favorite part of the poem is _____.

I would like to write another alphabet poem sometime. (Circle one.)

                    Yes   No

Teacher:

_____ correct format of poem

_____ appropriate word choice

_____ neatness

_____ correct spelling and mechanics

_____ _____

Score: _____

© Teacher Created Resources, Inc.   123   #2992 Poetry Writing—Grades 3–5

Phone Number Poem

Background for the Teacher

Definition: A phone number poem is a novelty poem in which the number of words in each line matches the numbers in a given phone number.

Skills Needed: no specific skills needed

Materials: reproductions of Phone Pattern (page 126) and Phone Number Poem Response and Assessment Sheet (page 128), colored construction paper, glue or tape

Preparation: Reproduce the Phone Number Poem Response and Assessment Sheet. Copy and trace the phone pattern on several pieces of tagboard or heavy construction paper and cut them out for students to use. Gather other materials needed for the lesson.

Lesson Plan

Prewriting

1. Read sample phone number poems to students.

2. Ask students to guess the structure of the poem. This will be a difficult task since the poems are about different topics and do not seem to follow the same structure.

3. Remind students that this type of poem is called a phone number poem. From that title, ask students to refine their ideas about the structure that these poems follow. You may need to assist students by counting the number of words in each line and asking if they have any new ideas.

4. Once students have figured out that the number of words in each line corresponds to the phone number digit, direct students to begin searching for a topic to use as their phone number poem. Students could use any topic that they generated during the fast-writes lesson (page 8), a topic from the Poet Tree (page 9), or any other idea that comes to mind. Encourage students to use a topic with which they have some familiarity since they may need to use many words about the topic in their poem.

Drafting

1. Have students write their phone number vertically on a sheet of paper, writing one number on every other line.

2. Instruct students to use the topic of their poem for the title.

3. Allow plenty of time for students to draft their phone number poem, writing only the number of words to correspond with their phone-number digit in each line.

Phone Number Poem *(cont.)*

Revising/Editing

1. When the poem is drafted, students should share their phone number poems with peer responders. Provide the Phone Number Poem Response and Assessment Sheet for this purpose. Peer responders should check to make sure that the title of the poem is the topic of the poem, that the correct number of words is included on each line, that the overall poem makes sense, and that the author has selected the best possible word choice.

2. Following peer response, students should make any necessary revisions before writing a final copy of the poem.

Publishing

1. Students could write the final copy of their phone number poem onto a plain piece of white paper, which could then be glued onto a tracing of the phone pattern where the number pad would be.

Student Samples of Phone Number Poems

Flying Free

(4)	I'd love to fly
(8)	With the birds and clouds in the sky
(2)	Soaring free
(4)	Just them and me
(8)	No chores to do, no veggies to eat
(4)	I'd sail up high
(5)	And land on my feet

Phone number: 482-4845

Too Short

(4)	Why is it that
(2)	I try
(2)	and try
(4)	and still I can't
(1)	shoot
(3)	a basketball in
(2)	the net?

Phone number: 422-4132

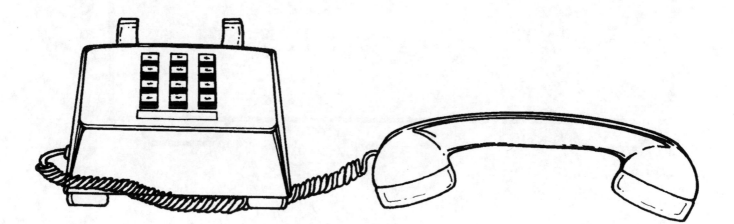

Phone Pattern

Directions: Make several copies of the phone pattern on tagboard and cut them out for students to use as a template for a background of their published poems.

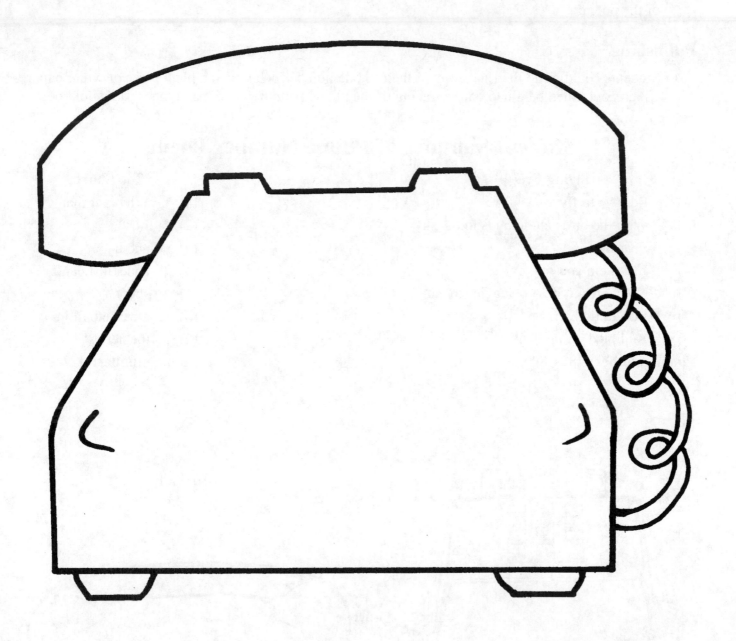

Content Connections for Poems Similar to Phone Poems

Suppose your social studies teacher has asked you to write about a year in history that you have been studying. Your teacher would like you to write a poem similar to a phone number poem to describe the year in history (in this case, it will be a "year poem"). A poem about 1776, for example, would have one word in the first line, seven words in the second and third lines, and six words in the last line. Think about the year in history you have been studying. Think about what happened during that time. Think about why certain things took place. Think about how the people during that time felt. Write a "year poem" describing the year in history that you have been studying.

Suppose your math teacher has asked you to write a poem using couplets that total a given sum. For example, if your teacher assigns the sum of 10, your couplets could contain three words on the first line and seven words on the second line for a total of ten words. Your next couplet could be six and four words or eight and two words, etc. Think of a topic for your "sum poem." Write at least three couplets that total the sum assigned to you.

Phone Number Poem Response and Assessment Sheet

Author's Name _____

Poem Title _____

Responder's Name(s) _____ Date _____

Responder:

Did the author . . .

❑ write the topic of the poem as the title?

❑ include the correct number of words on each line?

❑ connect the lines so that the overall poems makes sense?

❑ use the best possible word choice?

Revision suggestions: _____

_____

Author:

Before writing your final copy, have you . . .

❑ made any necessary revisions from your peer response session?

❑ checked for proper spelling?

❑ checked for proper capitalization?

❑ checked for proper punctuation?

Complete the following statements to provide some information about your writing:

I had a hard time _____

My favorite part of the poem is _____

I would like to write another phone number poem sometime. (Circle one.)

                     Yes   No

Teacher:

_____ correct format of poem

_____ appropriate word choice

_____ neatness

_____ correct spelling and mechanics

_____ _____

Score: _____

Two-Word Poem

Background for the Teacher

Definition: A two-word poem is a poem written with two words on each line. The subject of the poem could be anything. This lesson will teach students to write a two-word poem as a type of "character sketch" about a familiar person.

Skills Needed: no special skills needed

Materials: reproductions of the Here's Looking at You! worksheet (page 131), Two-Word Poem Response and Assessment Sheet (page 135), Photo Frame (page 132) for students to trace as necessary, photos of friends or family members of students, construction paper, glue or tape

Preparation: Reproduce the Here's Looking at You! worksheet, the Two-Word Poem Response and Assessment Sheet, and the Photo Frame for each student in the class. Ask students to bring a picture of a friend or family member to school in preparation for the lesson. Gather other materials needed for the lesson.

Lesson Plan

Prewriting

1. Have students place their pictures of their friend or family member on their desks. (See "Preparation," above.)

2. Distribute the Here's Looking at You! worksheet. Using the photograph as a reference, have students complete the worksheet to generate ideas for their two-word poem.

Drafting

1. Read the sample two-word poems to students.

2. Have students identify the structure of the poem (two words on every line).

3. Using the Here's Looking at You! worksheet as prewriting, have students draft a two-word poem about their chosen person. The title of the poem should be the name of the person. You may wish to establish a requirement regarding the number of lines to be included. This helps avoid the question, "How long does it have to be?"

Revising/Editing

1. When the poem is drafted, students should share their two-word poems with peer responders. Provide the Two-Word Poem Response and Assessment Sheet for this purpose. Peer responders should check to make sure that the title of the poem is the name of the person, that each line contains only two words, and that every line adds to the description of the person.

Two-Word Poem *(cont.)*

Revising/Editing *(cont.)*

2. Following peer response, students should make any necessary revisions before writing a final copy of the poem.

Publishing

1. Have students mount their photograph in a paper frame. If they create a double opening frame (using the Photo Frame for a model), students could mount the picture on one side and mount the poem on the other side.

Student Samples of Two-Word Poem

Cal Ripken, Jr.

Orioles shortstop
Now third
Number eight
Drinks milk
Plays everyday
Always ready
Signs autographs
Baseball legend
My hero

My mother

Tall, blond
English teacher
Funny, friendly
Nana's daughter
Strong, supportive
Role model
Loving mother
Best friend

Papa

My memories:
Going fishing
Peppermint candies
Making hamburgers
Watching baseball
Swinging slowly
Always interested
Always loving
Always Papa

Samantha

Little baby
Just born
Cries often
Drinks bottles
No hair
Cute face
Little fingers
Little toes
Love her

Here's Looking at You!

```
┌──────────────────────────────────┐
│                                  │
│                                  │
│                                  │
│                                  │
│      (Place photo here while     │
│           you work.)             │
│                                  │
│                                  │
│                                  │
│                                  │
└──────────────────────────────────┘
```

Answer the following questions about the person in your photograph.

What is the name of the person in your photograph?

_____

How do you know this person?

_____

What color hair does the person have?

_____

What color of eyes does the person have?

_____

Is this person tall, short, or average?

_____

Is this person heavy, thin, or average?

_____

How old is this person?

_____

What is this person's job?

_____

What does this person like to do in his or her free time?

_____

What do you like to do with this person?

_____

What do you like best about this person?

_____

Photo Frame

Use this as a template to make your own photo frame.

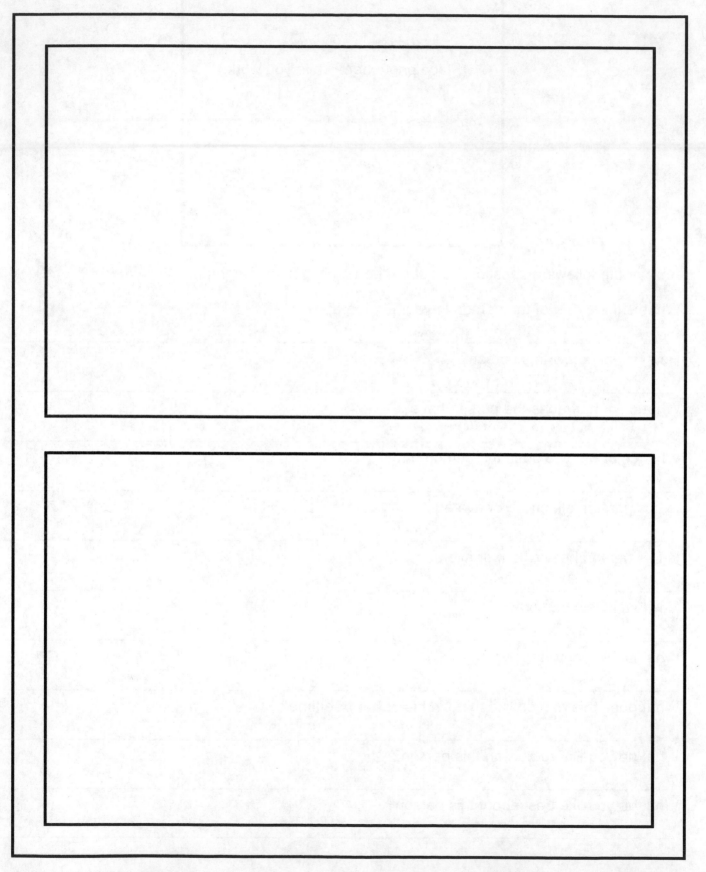

Content Connections for Two-Word Poems

Social Studies

Suppose your social studies teacher has asked you to describe a historical figure that you have been studying. Your teacher would like you to write a two-word poem to describe this person. Think about the person you have been studying. Think about what the person looks like. Think about why the person is important in history. Think about other information you know about the person. Write a two-word poem describing a historical figure that you have been studying.

Science

Suppose your science teacher has asked you to describe the traits of a plant or animal you have been studying. Your teacher would like you to write your description as a two-word poem. Think about the plant or animal you have been studying. Think about what it looks like. Think about where it lives. Think about other information you know about the plant or animal. Write a two-word poem describing the traits of a plant or animal you have been studying.

Content Connections for
Two-Word Poems *(cont.)*

Language Arts

Suppose your language arts teacher has asked you to describe a character in a story you have been reading. Your teacher would like you to write a two-word poem to describe this person. Think about the character in the story. Think about what the character looks like. Think about what the character does in the story. Think about other information you know about the character. Write a two-word poem describing a character in a story you have been reading.

Fine Arts

Suppose your art teacher has asked you to brainstorm different shades of basic colors (e.g., cornflower blue, sky blue, turquoise blue). Your teacher would like you to write a two-word poem about a basic color. Think about the assigned color. Think of different shades of the color. Think about objects that are the color. Write a two-word poem after brainstorming different shades of the assigned color.

Two-Word Poem Response and Assessment Sheet

Author's Name _____

Poem Title _____

Responder's Name(s) _____ Date _____

Responder:

Did the author . . .

❑ use the name of the person as the title of the poem?

❑ include only two words in each line?

❑ stay on the topic, writing only about the person in the photograph or their relation to that person?

❑ use the best possible word choice?

Revision suggestions: _____

_____

Author:

Before writing your final copy, have you . . .

❑ made any necessary revisions from your peer response session?

❑ checked for proper spelling?

❑ checked for proper capitalization?

❑ checked for proper punctuation?

Complete the following statements to provide some information about your writing:

I had a hard time _____.

My favorite part of the poem is _____.

I would like to write another two-word poem sometime. (Circle one.)

Yes   No

Teacher:

_____ correct format of poem

_____ appropriate word choice

_____ neatness

_____ correct spelling and mechanics

_____ _____

Score: _____

Acrostic Poem

Background for the Teacher

Definition: An acrostic poem is created by writing the title in capital letters vertically down the paper and using each letter to generate the content of a line of poetry. The first word in each line should begin with the corresponding letter from the title.

Skills Needed: no specific skills necessary

Materials: reproductions of Acrostic Poem Response and Assessment Sheet (page 140), alphabet stencils, markers or colored pencils

Preparation: Reproduce the Acrostic Poem Response and Assessment Sheet for each student in the class. Gather other materials needed for the lesson.

Lesson Plan

Prewriting

1. Ask students to jot down the name of their favorite movie or television show.

2. Have students brainstorm and list words related to the show—character names, places, adjectives, events, etc.

3. Instruct students to share their ideas about the show with a partner. If new ideas come to mind as they talk, encourage students to jot those down as well.

4. Read sample acrostic poems to students (page 137).

Drafting

1. Instruct students to write the title of their favorite movie or television show vertically on their piece of paper, using all capital letters.

2. Using their brainstormed list of related words, students draft the lines of their acrostic, starting each line with the corresponding letter from the title. Provide ample time for students to complete this draft.

Revising/Editing

1. When the poem is drafted, students should share their acrostic poem with peer responders. Provide the Acrostic Poem Response and Assessment Sheet for this purpose. Peer responders should check to ensure that each line begins with the correct letter and that all lines relate to the topic.

2. Following peer response, students should make any necessary revisions before writing a final copy of the poem.

Acrostic Poem (cont.)

Publishing

Allow students to use stencils to trace the first letter of each line. Students could decorate these letters using markers or colored pencils. Encourage students to decorate each letter in keeping with the topic of the poem.

For example, if a student's favorite show is *Star Trek*, the letter could be decorated with illustrations of planets, spaceships, meteors, etc.

Student Samples of Acrostic Poems

Boy, that dinosaur is annoying
Always singing in that whiny voice
Really, why do little kids like him?
Never have I seen a purple dinosaur
Everywhere I go someone's singing his songs.
Yikes! He's on TV right now!

Lazy
Impossibly difficult
Torture to their
    sisters
Too tough to handle
Loud and obnoxious
Every sister's
    nightmare

Brothers, who needs them?
Rude and disgusting
Oh, how I wish they would disappear
Their bratty little voices
Hard to bear
Easily, however, made to suffer
Remember—
Sisters are their worst nightmare!

Sand slipping through my fingers
Undertow pulling me into the cool
    ocean water
Multi-colored sunsets
Many days of sunshine
Everyone having fun
Radios blaring on the beach

Content Connections for Acrostic Poems

Suppose your social studies teacher has asked you to describe a historical figure that you have been studying. Your teacher would like you to write an acrostic poem to describe this person. Think about the person you have been studying. Think about what the person looks like. Think about why the person is important in history. Think about other information you know about the person. Write an acrostic poem describing a historical figure that you have been studying.

Suppose your science teacher has asked you to describe the features of a planet you have been studying. Your teacher would like you to write your description as an acrostic poem. Think about the planet you have been studying. Think about what it looks like. Think about where it is located. Think about its atmosphere. Think about other information you know about the planet. Write an acrostic poem describing the features of a planet you have been studying.

Content Connections for
Acrostic Poems *(cont.)*

Language Arts

Suppose your language arts teacher has asked you to describe a character in a story you have been reading. Your teacher would like you to write an acrostic poem to describe this character. Think about the character in the story. Think about what the character looks like. Think about what the character does in the story. Think about other information you know about the character. Write an acrostic poem describing a character in a story you have been reading.

Math

Suppose your math teacher has asked you to brainstorm vocabulary words from a unit you have been studying. Your teacher would like you to write your ideas as an acrostic poem, using the title of the unit for the first letters of the lines. Think about the unit you have been studying. Think of different words that relate to that unit. Think about phrases that provide information about the unit. Write an acrostic poem after brainstorming vocabulary words from a math unit you have been studying.

Acrostic Poem Response and Assessment Sheet

Author's Name _____

Poem Title_____

Responder's Name(s) _____ Date _____

Responder:

Did the author . . .

❑ begin each line with the correct letter?

❑ include only lines related to the topic?

❑ use the best possible word choice?

Revision suggestions: _____

_____

Author:

Before writing your final copy, have you . . .

❑ made any necessary revisions from your peer response session?

❑ checked for proper spelling?

❑ checked for proper capitalization?

❑ checked for proper punctuation?

Complete the following statements to provide some information about your writing:

I had a hard time _____.

My favorite part of the poem is _____.

I would like to write another acrostic poem sometime. (Circle one.)

Yes   No

Teacher:

_____ correct format of poem

_____ appropriate word choice

_____ neatness

_____ correct spelling and mechanics

_____ _____

Score: _____

Creating a Poetry Collection

Congratulations! You have completed a lot of hard work during this unit. You have written 18 different types of poems. Some poems were easy to write; some were harder. Some poems you are very proud of, while some poems you may want to revise again.

To celebrate your hard work, the last activity in our poetry unit is to organize your best or favorite poems into a personal poetry collection. To make this collection, you need to complete the following steps:

1. Select 15 of your best or favorite poems that you wrote during this unit.

2. Organize those poems into an order that makes sense to you. You may wish to include the poems exactly as you published them in class, or you may wish to use a word processing program on the computer to publish your poems in a different way. The final product is up to you!

3. Once you have organized your poems and have the final copies, obtain a table of contents from the teacher. For each poem you selected, complete the type and title of the poem on the Table of Contents. Also, include the page number of the poem as it will appear in your completed collection. Be sure to take into consideration any illustrations you may wish to include with your poems as you add page numbers.

4. Obtain a self-evaluation sheet from the teacher. Complete this worksheet and place it in your poetry collection as the very last page. (You do not need to include this in your Table of Contents.)

5. Create a title and cover page for your collection. You may simply call them ____(Your Name's)____ Poetry Collection or use your creativity and come up with another title. Some people like to use one of the titles of a poem as the title for the whole collection. Design and illustrate the cover page.

6. Bind your poetry collection in a folder or binder or hole-punch the pages and tie them with yarn or ribbon.

When students have completed their poetry collections, we will spend some time in class sharing our collections with other students.

Due Date _____

Table of Contents

Type of Poem	Title of Poem	Page	For teacher use only	
			Accuracy	Quality

Grading Criteria:

Fifteen different types of poems are included in the collection

Accuracy points:

3—The poem is written exactly according to directions.
2—The poem is written mostly according to directions.
1—The poem is written with little attention to directions.
0—The poem is not written following directions.

Quality points:

3—The poem is of high quality, using precise word choice, showing creativity, and including
   few or no mechanical errors.

2—The poem is of good quality, using appropriate word choice, showing creativity, and
   including few mechanical errors.

1—The poem is of average quality, showing little creativity, and may include many mechanical
   errors.

0—The poem is of poor quality, showing no creativity, and including many mechanical errors.

Poetry Collection Self-Evaluation Sheet

Author: _____

Title of Collection: _____

Self-Evaluation

1. Which poem in your collection do you like the best?

   _____

   Why? _____

   _____

   _____

   _____

2. Which poem was the hardest for you to write?

   _____

   Why? _____

   _____

   _____

3. Which poem was the easiest for you to write?

   _____

   Why? _____

   _____

   _____

Poetry Collection
Peer-Evaluation Sheet

Author: _____

Title of Collection: _____

Peer Evaluation

Peer Evaluator: _____

1. Which poem in this collection do you like the best?

   Why? _____

   _____

   _____

2. Write a comment of praise about the whole collection of poems.

   _____

   _____

   _____

3. Overall, how do you rate this collection on a scale of 1 (low) to 5 (high)? _____

   Why? _____

   _____

   _____

   _____

   _____

   _____